The View from Downshire Hill

The author

The View from Downshire Hill

A Memoir

Elizabeth Jenkins

MICHAEL RUSSELL

© Elizabeth Jenkins 2004

The right of Elizabeth Jenkins to be identified
as the author of this work has been asserted by her
in accordance with the Copyright, Designs
and Patents Act, 1988

First published in Great Britain 2004
By Michael Russell (Publishing) Ltd
Wilby Hall, Wilby, Norwich NR16 2JP

Typeset in Sabon by Waveney Typesetters
Wymondham, Norfolk
Printed and bound in Great Britain
By Biddles Ltd, King's Lynn, Norfolk

ISBN 0 85955 288 8

By the same author

FICTION

Virginia Water	1929
The Winters	1931
Portrait of an Actor	1933
Harriet *(Prix Femina Vie-Heureuse)*	1934
Doubtful Joy	1935
The Phoenix Nest	1936
Robert and Helen	1944
Young Enthusiasts	1947
The Tortoise and the Hare	1954
Brightness	1963
Honey	1968
A Silent Joy	1992

NON FICTION

Lady Caroline Lamb	1932
Jane Austen	1938
Henry Fielding	1947
Six Criminal Women	1949
Ten Fascinating Women	1955
Elizabeth the Great	1958
Elizabeth and Leicester	1961
Dr Gully	1972
The Mystery of King Arthur	1975
The Princes in the Tower	1978
The Shadow and the Light	1982

Contents

ॐ

Introduction

꒜

When she was in her early nineties, I urged my aunt Elizabeth Jenkins to write her memoirs. After some initial reluctance she finally decided to attempt an account of what she thought worth recalling from her childhood until the present day. The work is not intended to constitute an autobiography: indeed she once wrote that she did not believe she could ever keep a diary, adding that: 'I seem to be unable to put plain facts about myself down on paper without some form of distortion or synthetic colouring appearing.' What she has set down, therefore, is more a record of the impressions of people and places she has retained over a lifetime spanning virtually the whole of the twentieth century. Once she had set to work, she remarked that while she had difficulty recalling much of what had undoubtedly been important to her at the time, some distant or long forgotten episodes came back to her with startling clarity.

The work takes the form of numerous episodes in Elizabeth's life, together with anecdotes and reflections on her career as a writer. At Elizabeth's request I have sought to bring a chronological order to the material, but I have also excised a number of passages which tended to peter out either because of a failure of memory or on account of a conscious decision to hold back details which she felt uncomfortable about including. Rather than tantalise the reader it seemed better to omit these altogether. The thread of consistency running through the work is supplied by her voice: incisive, perceptive, humorous; but also self-deprecating and, if the phrase can be allowed, representative of a bygone age.

Elizabeth's long life has been, seen from the outside, relatively uneventful. She was born in 1905 in Hitchin, Hertfordshire, where her father had founded a preparatory school, and she was educated at a number of schools in the neighbourhood, including two in

Letchworth Garden City (as it was then known): a Methodist establishment, which she detested and from which she was hastily withdrawn, and a 'progressive' co-educational school, St Christopher's. From there she went up to Newnham College, Cambridge to study English, graduating in 1927. During her time at Cambridge she discovered her vocation as a writer. Her first book, a novel entitled *Virginia Water* (a love story based on an infatuation with a relative), was published shortly after she left Cambridge, and was favourably received; but she subsequently found the work embarrassing to the point where for a number of years she sought to exclude it from lists of her published books and would systematically buy and destroy any copies she could find. However, it cemented her relationship with Victor Gollancz who became both a friend and an invaluable mentor to her over a long writing career.

On leaving Cambridge, Elizabeth was introduced to Bloomsbury, and notably to Virginia Woolf, by the Principal of Newnham, Pernel Strachey (a sister of Lytton Strachey). She settled in London where she began to meet many of the literary figures of her day. Her father bought for her a small property in Hampstead – a Regency house in Downshire Hill – where she lived happily for the next fifty years in what one of her friends, the writer Elizabeth Bowen, described as 'rather threadbare elegance'. In the 1930s she published four novels and two biographies (of Lady Caroline Lamb and Jane Austen), so that by the outbreak of the war her reputation as a talented writer was firmly established. As the leading authority on Jane Austen she also became, in 1940, a founder member of the Jane Austen Society, to which she was to devote much time and effort in her later years. The most successful of the Thirties novels, *Harriet* (1934), was a gripping account of the slow but deliberate killing by starvation for her inheritance of a mentally retarded girl in the 1870s. Based on a true story, it was particularly well received and was awarded the prestigious Femina Vie-Heureuse literary prize, which was handed to her by E. M. Forster. Sadly, this book has long been out of print.

Elizabeth also spent some time in the Thirties teaching at another co-educational school, the King Alfred, in North London. Her experiences here, as well as at St Christopher's, were vividly described in what she called a 'reportage novel' which she published after the war, *Young Enthusiasts* (1947). She was remembered as an inspiring teacher of English literature, but the profession did not come naturally to her, and she ultimately concluded that 'so long as a living is to be made by scrubbing floors, nothing would induce me to work again in a school'.

During the Second World War Elizabeth remained in London and throughout the heavy bombing worked in several Government Departments. Her experiences, particularly in the then Ministry of Information, provide several entertaining passages in her memoir, but it is striking that no way was found to employ her in more senior positions for which she was intellectually undoubtedly qualified. Her modesty, unassuming manner and total lack of interest in directing events or exercising influence no doubt contributed to this.

In postwar years Elizabeth returned to full-time writing as a profession. Her total opus amounts to some twenty-three books, almost equally divided between novels and works of historical biography. The chief characteristics of her work have been an outstanding sense of period and place; and a profound understanding of women as either creators or victims of circumstance. Of her novels, the *Tortoise and the Hare* (1954) was, in the end, the most successful and is still widely read today: it was based on another love affair during which the man involved deserted her for a heavy, unattractive woman, who is vividly portrayed in the book. Her biography of Elizabeth I – *Elizabeth the Great* (1958) – was instantly recognised as a classic and much praised by leading Elizabethan historians such as A. L. Rowse. She has also had a lifelong interest in crime: she wrote about it extensively and was endlessly fascinated by the drama provided by criminal trials.

Apart from literature, Elizabeth's other passion has been the theatre. She has loved the company of actors and actresses and wrote a play for the actor Balliol Holloway, who became a close friend. The play was based on the relationship between Charles II and the Duke of Monmouth and after a successful run outside London, it was adapted and broadcast by the BBC.

Elizabeth has always been intensely private about her personal life. She is described in his diaries by A. L. Rowse, with whom she corresponded frequently for more than a decade, as 'so pretty she could have married twenty times over'. She undoubtedly formed a number of sentimental attachments, but her reluctance to marry may at least in part have been due, as she herself observes in this memoir, to an instinctive aversion to shouldering responsibility for another person's well being. As Elizabeth's writing career has come to an end she has relied increasingly on the company of a small group of friends to stimulate her interests. The premature deaths of her two brothers greatly saddened her: she has missed each of them intensely. But her cousin, John Guest, who shared many of her experiences of the 1940s and '50s, and various close friends have in recent years been happy to engage her in conversation, which for her is an art form in itself.

Diminutive in stature, Elizabeth Jenkins has penetrating blue eyes. There is about her an aura of iron-clad gentility, and she was once well described as being rather like her books, a combination of understatement and insight. But she will also be remembered by those who have know her for her sharpness of observation and humour, and by a wider public for the stylish and sensitive nature of her writing, whether in her fiction or non-fiction. Above all, with everything that she has said and written, Elizabeth is in her background and personality quintessentially English.

MICHAEL JENKINS

One

꙲

I and my two brothers, Romilly and David, were born in the first years of the last century at Brockton House in the Hertfordshire town of Hitchin. Built in 1866, the house was a fine example of the Victorian Gothic Revival: it had soft red brickwork and a brick and tiled lodge in the castellated style.

Both sides of my family had strong Methodist roots. My grandfather, Ebenezer Jenkins, had been a missionary in India in the 1840s where he acquired a formidable reputation as a preacher. There is a story in the family about Ebenezer which suggests a devotion to duty and honour more than befitting his ecclesiastical calling. Prior to his departure for India, he had taken lodgings in the house of a lady to whose niece he became attracted. After leaving for overseas he proposed marriage by letter and was accepted. It was agreed that the future bride would sail to India where the wedding would be celebrated. But when Ebenezer met the boat at the docks in Calcutta, it was not the niece who came down the gangway, but the aunt. The two ladies had the same name – Eliza Drewitt – and it was said that the letter had gone to the wrong one who had genuinely believed it was intended for her. Ebenezer's immediate reaction is not recorded; but he made the best of the situation and although she was a good deal older than he, married the senior Eliza. The marriage was a happy one, but there were no children and she died only a few years later.

On his return to England Ebenezer married into a prosperous North-Country Methodist family. My father, Ebenezer's only son, whose mother died giving birth to him, was sent to The Leys School in Cambridge, itself a Methodist foundation, where he subsequently became a junior master and then decided to found his own preparatory school as a 'feeder' for The Leys. On his marriage in

1903 he purchased the Brockton property and opened the school with eight pupils.

The school was named Caldicott because of a strange incident in my mother's family, whose name was Ingram. In the first half of the nineteenth century the heir to Caldicott Towers, an estate on the marches of Hereford, was the Caldicotts' son, a young man who made a voyage to Australia but was shipwrecked and presumed drowned. The Caldicotts' only surviving child was their daughter, Charlotte, the heiress presumptive of the estate, but on her parents' death it was impossible for her to claim it; her brother's death could not be proved as his remains had never been found. The estate therefore went into Chancery, where it remained, piling up riches.

Charlotte Caldicott was a member of a local Methodist community, where fervent religious conviction abolished all social distinctions, and she married, in 1837, a fellow member of the congregation, a local tradesman whose name was Ingram. In 1854 *Bleak House* was published, that dire object-lesson against having any dealings with the Court of Chancery as it then was. This, I dare say, hardened my great-grandfather's determination to have no ideas about the Caldicott estate; at all events his family were forbidden ever to mention the subject. One of them could just remember seeing him in the darkness of an early winter's morning, with a lantern in his hand, waiting to mount the stage-coach for London. He was thought to have called on a lawyer there, who advised against any action to claim the estate; but in spite of their expulsion from its grandeur, the Ingram family for several generations were given the name Caldicott among their forenames – my mother's name was Theodora Caldicott Ingram.

The most distinguished member of the Caldicott staff was Mr E. E. Kellett; he was older than my father, but they had been on The Leys staff together. Mr Kellett was very learned and an excellent teacher, the two qualities not always being found together. He came to Caldicott one afternoon a week to take Greek and Latin for the top form boys who wanted to sit the Common Entrance Examination, and he had tea in the drawing room afterwards. My mother had found out that he was particularly fond of blackberry (as distinct from blackcurrant) jam, and his tea was always the same: a boiled egg, followed by blackberry jam on brown bread and butter.

It was characteristic of my mother that she found out Mr Kellett's liking for blackberry jam. That the school remained well-fed during the 1914 war was due to her tireless housekeeping. In this she was powerfully supported by Moss's, the Hitchin grocers, whose name has been given to a local bus-stop, Moss's Corner. One of the boys' mothers told us how disappointed she'd been when she had managed to get for them something nice to eat which had become a rarity, and on seeing it, they had said: 'We've had that at Caldicott.' The dessert after school dinner on Sundays was a slice of pineapple and some Batger's Chinese figs. You could either eat the figs first, or keep them till they had soaked up the juice of the pineapple. A story in our family was of two young men meeting in the trenches, and discovering they'd both been to Caldicott. Their mutual question was: 'At Sunday dinner, did you eat your figs first, or the pineapple?'

At eight years old, I was dispatched to an educational establishment in Letchworth called The Modern School. This was one of the strangest episodes in my scholastic career, though it lasted only two terms. The headmistress, Miss Cartwright, was, I now realise, a typical feminist of the Shaw and Wells fashion; she was tall and gaunt, wearing spectacles and with white hair severely dressed. The school had quite a large number of day-girls, but very few boarders. These stuck it out for the term, but I was allowed to go home for weekends (which Miss Cartwright thought was a pity).

How I was sent to this school I don't know; I suppose it was hoped that by my mingling with the throng, I should develop a rather more intelligent and practical attitude to life. Letchworth was very cold, until you got used to it, after the shelter and warmth of Hitchin; the distance between the two ascended all the way, to a breezy upland. I've never known such cold as I experienced in that

dormitory. The beds had meagre blankets and starched linen coun-
terpanes. If you said you were cold, it was pointed out that you had
a 'footpad'. This was a square, also covered in glassy linen, and
lined in some substance about an inch thick. This, when laid over
your feet, was supposed to supply everything needed for health and
comfort. If I had not had that senseless characteristic common to
so many children, of not making a reasonable complaint to someone who would have put it right, I could have brought the eiderdown off my bed at home.

There were three mistresses, two of whom 'lived in' and were
bright and kind. The third, Miss Ellis, came daily; she was small
but valiant and high-principled to a degree. (When Lord Hugh
Cecil stood as Conservative candidate for Hitchin, Miss Ellis
called at his committee rooms and said to him: 'Your posters are
too inflammatory.') They all three made the lessons clear and
quite interesting, and if it hadn't been for the cold at night, I
would have found life tolerable, except that Miss Cartwright,
being quite free of debasing self-consciousness herself, made us
boarders do things we should never have been obliged to do. One
bleak winter term, the three mistresses, all pulling together, produced at Miss Cartwright's behest a collection of recitations,
songs, folk dances and playlets, all to be welded into one programme, which was to be offered to the general public at a local
hall. Presumably all the parents and Miss Cartwright's friends and
wellwishers bought tickets (some blue and, more expensive ones,
yellow) but besides this, and announcements in the local press, it
was felt desirable to hawk the tickets personally to houses in the
neighbourhood.

The streets near Norton Way were largely inhabited by factory
hands' families, who would not, one would think, want to put
down good money for this sort of entertainment, even in the pre-
radio and pre-television eras. Because we had to be back at school
for lessons at nine o'clock, the families we called on were disturbed
at their breakfasts; very good-natured they were, too, with warm
cheerful smells of frying bacon coming to the door with them, but

they did not buy any tickets. I felt extremely embarrassed at having to intrude on them with something they didn't want.

There was one boy among the boarders, Harold Langford, whose parents were in Africa. I was appointed on several occasions to go out with Harold on these harassing missions. It was winter; everything, soon after 8.30 a.m., was still wrapped in chill white mist, the grass verges were stiff with frost. Harold and I approached one of a pair of houses and our knock was answered by a gaunt, grey-haired woman in an apron who scowled fiercely at us, and when Harold asked if she would buy a ticket, her answer could hardly have been more indignant: it was a feat to express so much venom in so few words. We turned and ran back up the path; then we presented ourselves at the next front door. Here we had to knock and wait, and knock several times more. We were just about to make off when there was a heavy clanking and rattling of chains and the door shuddered and opened inwards: it was the elderly woman again! This time we didn't give here a chance to revile us, but turned tail and ran to the gate. It was many years before I came to see the comic side of this episode. I had merely accepted it as part of the sufferings.

By this time it was felt at home that I was not really profiting by the school's advantages, so I was taken away at the end of my second term. This was not the last of my contacts with Miss Cartwright, however. When my first novel was brought out she very kindly wrote to me, congratulating me on getting the work published and adding that she was sure that I would not write for 'self-glorification'. I replied as politely as I was able, but her letter raised a curious point: how *does* one write for 'self-glorification?' If I knew, I would be at it all the time. I dare say many of us would.

When I was twelve, I was already fascinated by the idea of Queen Elizabeth. One day my father said to me: 'At Odell's' (he named an excellent second-hand bookshop in the market square at Hitchin) 'they've got a copy of Mandell Creighton's *Queen Elizabeth*. They want two and six for it. I'll give you one and six, if you like to pay the shilling'. I have the book still. I have re-read it several times over the years with increasing comprehension and delight. This being so, I was intensely interested recently to read that is was Mandell Creighton who had given rise to Lord Acton's best-known saying.

Dr Creighton, then Bishop of London, was writing his history of the Papacy and he was anxious to be completely fair, not only as a conscientious historian, but so that no one should think that he, as an Anglican bishop, had been prejudiced against the Catholic Church. He said that though wickedness is always wickedness, in estimating the criminal's degree of guilt we must see it in the perspective of the era in which he lived. When the subject under consideration was the career of Pope Alexander VI, who, in private life, had been Count Rodrigo Borgia, the broad-minded but scrupulous historian was faced with some difficulty. However, Bishop Creighton attacked the task in his own method, and when copies of this first volume came off the press, he sent one to the Catholic Lord Acton – the leading historian of the day. Lord Acton's reply was unexpected. He found fault with Creighton for being too tolerant; he said that when every possible allowance had been made, and of course historical perspective demanded that it should be, there still remained 'an irreducible core of sheer wickedness', and, he added, 'You should have said so.' He did agree however that this condition was not surprising, as (and then immortal words rolled off this pen) 'power tends to corrupt, and absolute power corrupts absolutely'.

In 1924 I went to Newnham College in Cambridge to read for the English Tripos. I did realise how fortunate I was to be at Newnham, as I think everybody did; but life used one up to such an extent, at least in my case, that I could not realise the advantages then as profoundly as I do now.

Dr Leavis was, at that time, a person of might. I was not one of his students and I did not go to his lectures: the sort of study they required of you was above my head, and the little of his writings that I did understand seemed to me to demand a sort of grinding that took the excitement and joy out of poetry; but I must put down one extremely valuable gift that I acquired from him.

Newnham had a custom with certain students. As the date of the Tripos examination approached, they arranged for you to have one coaching with a lecturer whose student you were not: the idea being, no doubt, that if the man had taught you, you and he might be so much *en rapport* that he might, possibly, not be able to form a completely objective judgement of your work. A time was arranged for me to have a coaching with Dr Leavis, and he sent me a note, giving the title of the subject on which he agreed to read my essay. I cannot now remember what this was, but one thing I never forget is his crossing out about a third of one of the sheets of foolscap, and showing me how what he had left expressed my view much more forcibly than what I had originally written. I can't say I have invariably acted on this lesson, but I have at least always borne it in mind.

It was a considerable advantage to those of us reading English that F. L. Lucas was so thoroughly opposite to Dr Leavis in his considered views and reactions that between them they boxed the compass; Leavis being hypercritical, and scaling down what was worth reading to a startling minimum – no play of Shakespeare's, except *Othello*, no novel of Jane Austen's, except *Emma*, no *Faerie Queen*, no *Paradise Lost* at all – whereas F. L. Lucas thought so much of English Literature was marvellous: he encouraged you to read, and read, to light up the wonder and delight he felt himself.

Another Cambridge scholar to whom I have always felt deeply indebted was H.S. Bennet. In small coaching groups he taught one so much about Shakespeare that, after A. L. Rowse, no one was his equal. It was he who pointed out that the Elizabethan idea of king-ship (or of monarchy, as the views of the theatre-going public were influenced by the enormous personal success of Queen Elizabeth) was so overpowering that Shakespeare inflicted a disability on all of the monarchs (with one exception), to bring the roles within the actors' reach: John dies in agonies of poisoning, Richard II is a poetic weakling, Henry IV is tormented by insomnia, Richard III is a hunchback, King Lear insane. The exception, Henry V, was such a national hero that the audience would not have allowed any diminishing of him. Burbage just had to do the best he could.

The other outstanding actor, the star of The Lord Admiral's Company, the rival to Shakespeare's Lord Chamberlain's, was Edward Alleyn, who made a fortune and endowed Alleyn's School, now Dulwich College. Mr Bennet reminded us how Shakespeare took him off in Hamlet's instructions to the players as to how *not* to act (Alleyn wore a curled wig and Hamlet said it infuriated him, to see 'a periwig-pated fellow' stamping about the stage in such an unnatural manner, it looked as if one of Nature's apprentices had tried to create a man, and made a bad job of it); but there was another allusion to Alleyn, Mr Bennet said, in *A Midsummer Night's Dream*, where Bottom wants to take all the parts himself. In spite of this satirical treatment at Shakespeare's hands, I was fascinated by the idea of Edward Alleyn; not the equal of Burbage, but an immensely successful and popular actor, who combined height with physical charisma. Edward Thomas said in the preface to the Everyman Edition of Marlowe's plays: '*Tamburlaine* is all action ... it could only reach its highest form of life with the aid of actors and a stage.'

I went several times to the Dulwich Picture Gallery to look at Alleyn's portrait, of which his face, as an actor's, is striking, but the full-length figure is somewhat disappointing – Alleyn having been very tall, the painter appears to have sacrificed a small part of the height to get the feet on to the canvas. Nonetheless, the effect is highly impressive, and on my visits I always made for the place on the wall where the portrait hung. To my acute disappointment I was once met by a stupefying blank. I ran after the custodian, whom I saw disappearing through one of the exits, and begged him to explain. He said the school had had an important anniversary some time ago, and had asked the gallery to lend them this portrait of their Founder. He added: 'We have reminded them, once or twice, that we should be glad to have it returned, but so far they haven't been able to send it back.' I could have retorted, 'Of course they haven't been able to send it back! What could you expect?' The impulse was momentary; to give way to it would have been not only rude, but wanting in sympathy. The portrait of their Founder must have cut such a fine figure as the centrepiece of the school's exhibition, which displayed the manager Philip Henslowe's account-book, containing a list of Alleyn's costume when he played in *Tamburlaine the Great* – 'Tamburlaine his black velvet cloak, Tamburlaine his crimson satin breeches' – and Alleyn's part in *Orlando Furioso*, which is written out, with cues, on strips of paper pasted together, the whole length rolled round a spindle so that he could unroll it when getting it by heart. The portrait, needless to say, has been returned long since.

Alleyn's third wife was the daughter of the poet John Donne, and anyone who has found the style of Donne's poetry sometimes rather daunting will feel for Alleyn when, at a critical stage in the arrangements for the marriage settlement, he wrote Donne a letter saying 'I pray you, understand a plain man in his plain meaning.' All the inspiring interest of this area I associate with Mr Bennet.

I suppose it would have been in 1926; I was the secretary of the Newnham Literary Society and we invited Edith Sitwell to address us. This meant that I had to ask to speak to our Principal, Miss Strachey, as the lecturer would be her guest for the night. Miss Strachey, to know whom, even slightly, was one of the experiences of a life-time, was reserved but completely amiable in the matter. Edith Sitwell's fame rested not only on her poetry, but on the impression of her personal appearances. In an era when female dress consisted of cropped hair, knee-length skirts and cloche hats, she wore *robes de style* of rich colours, and rings bearing aquamarines and topazes the size of prunes. As it was my duty to write the invitation, I said to Miss Strachey: 'Shall we say: "Please wear everything you've got"?' Miss Strachey said gently: 'I don't *think* that will be necessary.'

Nor was it; Edith Sitwell's appearance satisfied every possible expectation. Her very tall, slight figure, with the long oval face, the delicately aquiline nose and the domed eyebrows were familiar from photographs; the dress in which she appeared was high-necked, long-sleeved, with a wide, floor-length skirt of grass-green brocade embroidered with gold palm leaves, and she had enormous aquamarines on her fabulously long fingers. In one of her early poems she had said of herself and her two brothers: 'We all have the remote air of a legend.'

I cannot now remember which of her poems she read to us, and I dare say many of them I wouldn't have been able to follow in any case, but I've never forgotten one thing she said, which was my first realisation that whether one enjoyed her own poems or not, she was exceptionally interesting in what she said about the poetry of other people. She related to us on this occasion how she had been viciously derided in the press for lines in one of her poems:

> ... a crude, fish-tinsel pink
> That flapped across the consciousness like laughter.

The critics had been angry because she used the sensation received by one sense to describe the sensation received by another; but, she said, had not Dante done the same, when he spoke of 'a place, dumb of light'? (I was reminded of this many years later as I read of Dom Perignon's exclamation, when he had invented sparkling champagne – 'I am drinking stars!')

I was kindly summoned by Miss Strachey next morning to say goodbye to Edith Sitwell, and this was the origin of my being able to see her, at intervals, over the next decades. She remained an object of fascination to me. Her conversation was as absorbing as it was unpredictable. She talked with a weird, elemental creaking yet graceful malice – uniquely original and with bursts of high voltage pantomime humour.

In 1925 Miss Strachey's brother, Lytton Strachey, had given the Leslie Stephen lecture on Alexander Pope, and now, in my hearing, Edith Sitwell gave Miss Strachey her tribute to Lytton Strachey's brilliant appreciation. How tragic and pitiable it was, she added, that a man who wrote as Pope wrote, with such airiness and vigour, was hump-backed and deformed. 'He ought to have walked like

Nijinsky,' she said. I had not then seen Nijinksy, but one knew of his amazing feat of being able to perform ten *entrechats* in mid-air: two being the usual achievement of a dancer, and five outstandingly good. Nijinsky, it was said, was actually balancing in mid-air as he crossed and recrossed his ankles ten times before coming down on stage again. This evocation of Nijinsky's supernatural agility and grace, called up by association with Pope's poetry, is an evidence of the faculty ascribed to Edith Sitwell by Elizabeth Salter in her biography: 'her awareness of the inter-connection of everything within the whole of creation.'

Interesting as I thought Edith Sitwell's poetry was, much of it was obscure to me. It was her brother Sacheverell whose work gave me the keenest delight. In his collection of poems entitled *The Thirteenth Caesar* there is a 'Variation on a theme by Alexander Pope' which is based on Book XI of Pope's translation of *The Odyssey*. Odysseus visits the abode of the dead, and through the darkness recognises the armed figure of Achilles. The hero of the Trojan Wars says that if he could only come back to the living world, he would willingly return in the status of slave; but that he would be comforted even here, if he could know that his son, Neoptolemus, was successful and eminent. Odysseus tells the father that his son is an admired orator, and the famous hero of the final attack on Troy from the belly of the Trojan horse. Achilles is delighted to hear of his son's renown.

> With haughty stalk he sought the distant glades
> Of warrior kings, and joined the illustrious shades….

Sacheverell Sitwell's variation is:

> Far down in the myrtle grove
> Wander the youths who died for love
> And the hero's armèd shade
> Glitters down the gloomy glade.

This has always seemed to me hauntingly beautiful.

I met Sacheverell once at one of Edith Sitwell's parties when she was living in Hampstead. He told me that, one wet Sunday afternoon when Charing Cross Road looked empty, he was walking down it towards Trafalgar Square when he saw Chaliapin, who was immediately recognisable, coming towards him on the opposite side of the road (it was during a season when Chaliapin was singing at Covent Garden). As Chaliapin drew level with the statue of Irving, he raised his hat and bowed slightly. Sacheverell said he had no idea of playing to an audience: in the empty street, he did not think anyone saw him.

The tutor of Newnham's Peile Hall, Helen Palmer, was the sister of Henry Lamb; to this we owed the fact that in 1927 he painted the portrait of Miss Strachey as the Principal of Newnham. It is unique among the College's collection of solid but uninteresting Victorian portraits and contemporary but unimpressive ones of modern Principals.

Henry Lamb's portrait of Lytton Strachey, now in the Tate Gallery, is a wonderful piece of work, but with its length and limpness of limb, it appears to verge on caricature. In his portrait of Miss Strachey, the strangeness and the magic are all there, but do not exceed those qualities in the original.

Lamb said in a letter to a friend that he was preparing his studio for the sittings, and meant to bring in another paraffin stove so that 'the dear lady' should not feel cold. This causes a faint smile in anyone who remembers how acutely Miss Strachey did feel the cold, and how, at the prospect of a visit from her to coffee in the winter term, it was felt necessary to stoke the coal fire (with which the rooms were then provided) almost up to the ceiling, from teatime onwards.

During my time at Newnham the study of Marxism and the social experiment represented by the Soviet Union became increasingly fashionable, as it was to remain with many intellectuals throughout the 1930s. As far as I read any Marxist works, or was personally acquainted with Communist intellectuals, they seemed to me like Compton Delville in Fanny Burney's *Cecilia*, 'arrogant

[24]

without merit, imperious without capacity'. One of the best things I have heard any of them say was apropos of André Gide, who, it was known, after a visit to the USSR, had resigned from the Communist Party. As soon as this was mentioned, a young man, very pale, squeaky-voiced and superior, exclaimed: 'People quite often do that; they find the intellectual pace of Marxism too much for them.' I never met André Gide, but *Les Faux Monnayeurs* was the most exciting modern novel I ever read. It had the effect of making one into an adult at one coup but the intellectual pace of Marxism, one had to understand, spared nobody.

I recall one student at Newnham, very strongly Communist, who much wanted to go to London, on May 1, to attend the celebrations and rejoicings in Hyde Park. When she applied for leave, however, her tutor told her that no leave was being given that week, as it was so near the sittings of the Tripos. The girl would not take no for an answer, and insisted on seeing Miss Strachey to put her case. Miss Strachey said to her: 'You are quite intelligent enough to understand that an institution like this one can't be run without some sort of discipline. *Your* party takes discipline very seriously; in fact, if they come to power, I myself should be quite probably be shot.' The girl exclaimed eagerly: 'Oh, but that would only be in the transition period!'

Two

As I was going down from Newnham, Miss Strachey asked me, with her usual detached elegance, if I would like an introduction to Virginia Woolf? It seemed to me, at the time, that life could afford no more exciting prospect. I was almost speechless. She added, encouragingly: 'She's always asking me why I don't send her any of my young ladies.' However speechless, my enthusiasm and gratitude must have made themselves plain, for she then gently added that people in Bloomsbury Society were apt, sometimes, to be rather unkind in what they said. I exclaimed that I was sure I should not mind that. She had given me the warning, but nothing was going to prevent my rushing towards the precipice.

On leaving Newnham, I had a year in London before looking for a post. I had no definite occupation, but I found my way to the Reading Room, as it was then called, in the British Museum. I acquainted myself with bus routes and the underground railway; every day was an exploration of roads and streets and of what was going on in my mind. I was writing my first novel, which I called *Virginia Water*, an absurdly *surrealistic* title, but I don't know that it was any more absurd than the contents of the work. However, writing it absorbed me profoundly. I have never written anything that I have not loved writing; no written work has ever been a bore to me, though often surrounded by difficulties. But this book occupied me in a way that was different from anything that I have ever done since. The later things were, in a way, more interesting, but they were different; perhaps many people would say they had had the same experience with a first novel.

My parents took a small furnished bed-sitting room for me in a lodging-house in Doughty Street, between Brunswick Square and Bedford Square. In those days, unaltered by air-raid damage and modern improvements, the district presented long façades of brick frontages and regular rows of sash-windows. Doughty Street was in a similar condition to the plain and graceful London of the early 1800s.

Mrs Woolf's simple note arrived, asking me, if I were free, to come to them on Thursday evening after dinner. The address was Tavistock Square, within easy walking distance of Doughty Street. As her subsequent invitations were all of the same kind, my recollection of them begins with going on foot, through the dusk and silence of Doughty Street, through the brisk modern cheerfulness of Russell Square, to the gloom, once more, of Bedford Square, where a bust of one of the Dukes of Bedford stood on a plinth in its gardens, under sweeping boughs.

Tavistock Square, of later date than the other Bloomsbury squares, had a many-windowed, lofty brick frontage. The Woolfs occupied a flat on one of the upper floors, and Leonard Woolf himself came down the stairs to let me in. His gentle kindness, his simplicity and his distinction made an unforgettable impression on me, which never altered. He and Mrs Woolf were alone in a sitting room on the upper floor. The furniture was covered in worn cretonne upholstery, the walls were painted in a series of latticed arches, done, as I afterwards heard, by Mrs Woolf's sister, Vanessa Bell, in the curious idiom, hyper-fashionable at the time, of a startling absence of perspective, and a sort of staggering crookedness. There were lighted candles on the mantelpiece and their light was strengthened by the glow of a large coal fire.

Virginia Woolf was tall and angular. Her face, despite a slightly exaggerated length, was very beautiful. Her nose was delicately aquiline, her eyes, a bluish grey, very large and deep-set. At that time she was wearing her silvery-grey hair brushed back from her forehead and pushed behind her ears, reaching half-way down her neck. It was an era when skirts were very short, and her extended legs were exposed, stretched out, long and fragile, like stems of old-fashioned clay pipes. I was struck at once by her dignity and grace, and her complete lack of self-consciousness.

[27]

The small comfortable room with its ineffably distinguished occupants was enough to take one's breath away. Mine almost went, though not without sensations of pleasure. But I have no doubt that I was more naïve and gauche than at any other time of my life.

The conversation was not exactly interesting in itself, but of extreme interest because it was uttered by *them*. Some of it concerned young people who had left home to be independent but were struggling to make ends meet. Suddenly Mrs Woolf said, with an introspective stare, as if she were looking at something under glass: 'Are you *poor*, Miss Jenkins?' Searching for an appropriate reply, I said 'Well, not necessitous' and they both burst out laughing.

Quite often these invitations, which arrived once every few weeks, were to the Woolfs by themselves, occasions particularly enjoyable and gratifying; others included people I had never heard of, as well as those whose names were familiar, such as Miss Strachey's brothers, Oliver and James. Lytton Strachey, who was then at the height of his fame, was too sacred to be met casually, though I did, in fact, once meet him *à l'improviste* when Miss Strachey had asked me to tea with her at the family house in Gordon Square, where he had a flat. He arrived unexpectedly on his return from a visit to Cambridge, and came in to have tea with his sister instead of making it for himself. Talking of his Cambridge visit, he said to her, apologetically: 'Parties were so thick I couldn't reach you.' The Three Arts Ball was coming up, and he asked me if I were going. As it happened, I was. He said: 'And what will you wear?' I said that someone had lent me an 1830 yellow brocade dress, very full in the sleeves and off the shoulders. He breathed 'Marvellous!' in a tone of quiet satisfaction. I never saw him again, but have always felt that, considering everything, this brief exchange could hardly have been improved on.

I do not remember how long my term of visiting in Tavistock Square lasted, a matter of months I think. On one occasion there was some discussion of an experimental kind of writing. Mrs Woolf turned to me and said: 'Why don't *you* try it, Miss Jenkins?' I said nothing, I supposed I looked suitably shy. I didn't like to say I was already working very hard on a novel. On that same evening I was surprised by an indication of how very much Virginia Woolf resented, was wounded even, by adverse criticism, even of a kind to which one would have expected her to be impervious. A current weekly had carried an unfavourable comment on her work by E. F. Benson. The station-master at Rodmell, the station for the Woolfs' country house, had put a copy into her hand, saying 'Something here to interest you, madam'. She now commented on the article to the assembled guests, adding: 'Perhaps poor E.F. feels that he's being left behind? Do you think so?' Her contemptuous, unnaturally high tone of voice seemed to show an unexpected degree of pique and annoyance in someone so distinguished.

The last time I visited Tavistock Square was an unfortunate justification of Miss Strachey's warning which I had so confidently brushed aside. On this occasion there was present a charming girl, very courteous, very much pleased to be there, but with all the unthinking self-confidence of aristocratic, as distinct from intellectual, tone. She spoke of the Paget twins, and asked if Mrs Woolf knew them. The latter said, respectfully, only from mentions in the newspapers. In the meantime I was silent; I was not spoken to and there was no facet of the conversation to which I could spontaneously contribute.

I was of course there by Mrs Woolf's invitation, but she was now treating my presence as a rather tiresome misfortune. She did not, however, entirely ignore me; a few remarks were launched in my direction, slight but painful, but strange to say I have so successfully performed a kind of mental blackout of the occasion that I cannot remember the words, only the tone of her voice, contemptuous and mocking, as she produced them. I do remember Leonard Woolf's accompanying me downstairs to the front door with undemonstrative kindness.

I felt sore and laid-to-waste, though not for long. I did not attempt to regain Mrs Woolf's notice, though I heard through a mutual acquaintance that she had spoken about me to him, saying that she had not seen me for some time and asking if I had left London. I worked very hard to finish my novel, and at the end of the year I obtained a post as senior English mistress at the King Alfred School in North London, a co-educational school, which provided a scene of varied and stimulating experience. They were very good to me and arranged for my work to be put into the mornings so that I had the afternoons free. I held this post for ten years until, at the onset of the war in 1939, the school was transplanted to Royston in Hertfordshire, and I, being at large, was seized upon and put into three Government offices in succession.

Meantime I had finished my novel, *Virginia Water*, and sent it to Victor Gollancz, whose name I knew because of his enormous advertisements in the Sunday papers. I was extremely fortunate in that the first publisher to whom I sent it proved to be the one who was going to take it. I could, like many other people, have gone in the contrary direction, and begun on a list of firms who would have rejected it.

Victor asked me to come and see him in his premises at Henrietta Street, Covent Garden, where I scrambled up a flight of attic stairs to the small room where Victor sat at this desk – large, impressive, kind and formidable. He said: 'You've done a good deal of writing?'

'No,' I said, 'only this.'

'You mean you've done other things, but scrapped them?'

'No,' I said, 'this is all I've ever done.'

He made a half-turn and took a printed contract form out of one of the drawers of his desk. He then made his offer, an advance of £60, which, in money of the time, and to such as me, was perfectly acceptable. He explained that the contract would give him the first refusal of my next three books. He then asked if I would sign it.

'Yes,' I said.

He said: 'We'll get someone downstairs to witness it', adding: 'It's not *selon les règles* to have it signed and witnessed in the office, but perhaps it won't matter.' I said 'I'm sure it won't.' I nearly snatched from his fingers the pen he was offering me.

The novel was a success, and I was fortunate in reviews; altogether it widened my circle very much. I did not see Virginia Woolf again. She did not give me another invitation, and I did not feel equal to proposing myself, though I heard, through Alan Clutton Brock, that she had found out that we knew each other and had asked him how I was getting on.

Many years afterwards, I read the posthumously printed volumes of her diaries, and under the appropriate year I saw that she had noted my novel as 'a sweet white grape of a book'. This was, in one way, a relief and satisfaction; she could easily have referred to it with scorn, or omitted any reference to it at all. But in spite of my pleasure, I could see that her critical acumen had led her to put her finger on my inherent weakness: a lack of strength. This has always, I fear, come out in any novel I have written purely by imagination; a fictional version of a real story of real life, a transcript of experience or a straightforward biography, has been needed to supply my deficiency.

For almost all of my working life I was able to spend uncounted hours in the British Museum, having obtained a reader's ticket in my twenties and renewed it at stated intervals until my handbag, which contained it, was stolen in 1995. I wrote ten or more novels, but all my other books were biographies, for which, of course, I depended completely on the Reading Room: on the books indexed in the circle of catalogues in the centre of the room, and on those on the open shelves. The sharp thing was to arrive very early and install yourself on a seat at the end of the rows, radiating out from the central desk, where the staff presided; this situation put you within a few paces of the open shelves which lined the circular hall. The books on these included dictionaries of biography, collections of letters, volumes of standard histories and, above all, the Catalogues of State Papers.

The first biography I wrote was of Lady Caroline Lamb, which Victor Gollancz published in 1932. It was an extraordinary fact that though this bewitching creature was mentioned in letters and biographies without number, no one before me had devoted a whole book to her. I have already said how fortunate I was that the King Alfred School put all my work into the mornings, so that I was free from one o'clock. I was able therefore to get down to the Reading Room by three o'clock, and stay there till they closed at six. I poured myself into this work.

Melbourne House in Whitehall, the town house of Lord and Lady Melbourne, the parents-in-law of Lady Caroline, where she and William Lamb had an apartment on one of the upper floors, was then in the possession of the War Office, and one could get permission to see over it. The book had a considerable success, created by the lively attraction of the period and of the central figure; but although I still feel that Lady Caroline had an extraordinary charm, I could never now write with so much sympathy about such a character. Over the years we have, so many of us, seen too much of selfish neurotics who damage other people's lives; but I suppose that over half a century ago this state of affairs was not so prominent in society as it is now. I had been obliged to write to the late Lord Ponsonby to find out whose permission I should ask to quote some of the family letters. When I sent him a copy of the published work, he wrote to me saying 'Your bricks were rather few and scattered but your mortar is so good.' This from a collateral descendant was very gratifying; and hearing that the invaluable Mr H. S. Bennet had read it and said that it was a 'very beautiful and sensitive piece of work', even more so. I naturally exulted, as who would not, but I do now wonder how much Lady Caroline's hyper-thyroid behaviour he would have put up with himself!

When in 1921 my parents retired from Caldicott and moved to Letchworth, I never ceased to think of Hitchin, the home of my childhood, with romantic affection. Though much defaced, it was still a pretty country town when we left it. The Hiz, a river too small to appear in atlases, shows itself at intervals in the town, one reach of it skirting the parish church of St Mary's, where, sherry-coloured, it moves briskly along over pebbles like cobblestones.

My brother David had a successful career in London as a solicitor, but he began it in Hitchin, articled to the firm Hawkins and Co, which occupied a charming Georgian building in Portmill Lane, a quiet street. Of the three partners, Reginald Hine was more distinguished as an antiquarian and local historian than as a lawyer, as the other two partners, Arthur Lindsell and Bill Times, were sometimes heard to murmur when faced with the extra work which Mr Hine, in his historical researches, was obliged to leave on their hands. However, the firm was a friendly one in which to work and David's connection with it brought me an unexpected opening. The firm had been founded in the early nineteenth century by a Mr Hawkins, whose son, Henry Hawkins, had a spectacular career at the bar: first, in the famous Tichborne case, in which an impostor claimed that he was Roger Tichborne, a young man who had been drowned in a shipwreck. The impostor's claims, producing witnesses from the other side of the globe and covering a stretch of years, required extraordinary powers of collection and arrangement to defeat them. Having lost his case, he was arrested and tried for perjury, and Hawkins, who led for the Crown, made such an impression that he was offered a judgeship, which he first refused as, after an agonisingly slow start, he was now enjoying the position of a counsel whose services were being clamoured for. But when the judgeship was offered to him again, he did not think it right to refuse. The first case to come before him in 1877 was, he said, 'the most sensational case I was called upon to preside over'. This was the trial of the Stauntons, known as the Penge Case.

It was a crime involving almost unbelievable callousness and cruelty. A half-witted young woman named Harriet who had inherited a small fortune was living happily and securely in the care of her mother. Lewis Staunton, a good-looking young man and a relentless criminal, saw his opportunity, and making love to the innocent, ignorant creature, got her away from her mother's protection and married her. He then arranged for her to be boarded with his brother Patrick Staunton and the latter's wife Elizabeth, while he set up house with his mistress, Elizabeth's sister, Alice. All this went on in the Kentish village of Cudham. The most horrible feature of the case was slow starvation by neglect of Harriet and her baby. She was kept in a fireless room with half the window boarded up, despite the frantic efforts of her mother to reach her. The baby died, and she herself was nearly dead when she was taken by the three Stauntons to Penge. Here the services of a nurse were engaged, but the victim, emaciated and filthy, died within a few hours. The Stauntons tried to have her buried immediately, but the doctor who was asked to sign the death certificate demanded a coroner's inquest. This brought on an inquiry and finally the trial.

The three Stauntons and Alice were charged with murder but Hawkins pointed out to the jury that though Lewis Staunton, as the victim's husband, was responsible for her well-being, and his brother and sister-in-law were responsible for her keep as they were being paid for it, Alice, as the mistress, had no legal responsibility for the wife; if she were an accomplice in the death, at most she would be guilty of manslaughter. But in spite of this encouragement to discrimination, the effect on the jury of his summing-up was so powerful – he did not conclude it till quarter to ten at night – that the jurors, beside themselves, brought in all four prisoners guilty of murder, though they recommended Alice to mercy. The reaction was that the Home Secretary freed Alice and reprieved the other three, but visited them with long terms of penal servitude.

The case was a nine days' wonder. The story was told in Hertfordshire that when some years later Sir Henry Hawkins and a friend, after a walk in the fields, went into a pub for drinks, the barmaid said 'That'll be eightpence to you, my lord.' He said 'Why, do you know me?' She said 'I ought to: you sentenced me to death'; and this was Alice.

The case was later included in that superb series, *Notable British Trials*, and a copy was lodged in the office of Hawkins and Co. My brother lent it to me, and I was completely absorbed by it. In 1934 I wrote the story, which I called by the victim's name, *Harriet*. I would not work on such a theme now – I could not face imagining such horrors; but then we, the public, had not yet heard the details of the Nazi concentration camps. The book was, however, a success, and it was, I think, one of the very earliest instances – if not the earliest – of a writer's recounting a story of real life, with the actual Christian names of the protagonists and all the available biographical details, but with the imaginative insight and heightened colour which the novelist exists to supply.

Where I departed from the original, because the psychological material was not there, I made all four of the actors too sensitive: by visualising Elizabeth's loyalty to her husband as a passionate absorption, and crediting the two brothers with a sort of heroic partisanship for each other, I gave the sordid tale an interest which I now see it never had. Perhaps in the interest of the story it was an allowable exaggeration; but where I went absurdly amiss was in the evocation of Alice. These were, however, the 1930s, the era of keen interest in the British film industry; it was necessary to present her as potently attractive sexually, to Lewis at least, and I envisaged her, though criminally selfish and limited, with a glamour that would have got her an audition at the Elstree studios. This was preposterous overpainting.

The book was my first commercial success, which naturally was exciting, but two aspects of the matter were agitating. First, the horror of the story weighed on my mind and became more acutely painful as time went on; as I have said, I would not now ever consider treating such a subject. Then, though most of the reviews were generous, a few vindictive ones made me understand, for the first time, that in making use of an actual story, though of a past era, and keeping the names of people and place intact, I had done something considered by some people as highly blameworthy: a sort of flagrant breach of copyright. If the book had fallen flat with the press, this would not have worried them, but a success by a relatively unknown author in this hitherto unexploited genre was too much. A reviewer in the then-running weekly *Time and Tide*, who signed himself A. B. Cox (though I believe this was a *nom de plume*), exposed this piece of literary malpractice by listing the characters in my book against their names in real life; I had almost always kept the Christian names but altered the surname. I confess that it had never occurred to me that anyone would think what I had done discreditable. I never thought about the matter, one way or the other. I had been obsessed by the story and the powerful current of energy that enabled me to write it. Since then, numerous writers have followed this method.

There was one fascinating tailpiece. I had a letter from an old lady, Mrs Akins, living in the neighbourhood of Luton, which said 'I think your story must be about the family that I was in service with when I was a young girl.' We arranged a meeting and Mrs Akins received me in the most kind and friendly way in her little house. Patrick Staunton had died in gaol, and at the end of her sentence his widow had established herself as the proprietress of a set of rooms which she called Llewellyn Chambers (her husband's name had been Patrick Llewellyn Staunton), used largely by officers on leave from the Boer War. Mrs Akins had been one of six or eight housemaids. Elizabeth married again, to an old man who was no doubt the owner of the chambers. It was Mrs Akins's duty to take him up a bowl of soup in his bedroom in the middle of the morning. One day she was a little late, and as she came in with the soup he did not see her because there was a screen across the foot of the bed, but she heard him muttering 'I shall get up. *I'm* not going to stay up here and be starved!' And she said it wasn't till she read my book, so many years later, that she realised what those words had meant.

Elizabeth was quite good-natured as an employer but Mrs Akins had been puzzled by her sometimes walking up and down, nursing her arm as if it hurt her and repeating, 'What have I done to deserve this? What have I done to deserve this?' When she asked the other maids about it, one of them said 'She got cold in it when she was in prison.' Here Mrs Akins said feelingly: 'When you go into service, they ask about *your* character – you never get the chance to hear about *theirs*!'

She had one other glimpse of the Staunton family, though, again, she did not see the force of it till she read the book. One day she was hurrying upstairs after midday dinner, to change into her 'blacks', and at the head of the staircase she passed a man who was standing there, sunburned with grey hair and whiskers. When she got into the maid's dormitory she exclaimed 'I've just passed a nasty-looking man on the stairs – he gave me such a nasty look.'. The others told her: 'That's the mistress's brother-in-law – *he's* done twenty years in a gaol'; and this was Lewis! It was all living to her still, some thirty-six years afterwards. Altogether a most rewarding afternoon, the only disappointment being that she could tell me nothing about Alice, except that she had gone to settle in Canada. Yes, Mrs Akins said, there had been a photograph of her among the mistress's things, but she could remember nothing about her: not even if she was fair or dark. This caused me a momentary pang but I have realised long since that any photograph of Alice, though interesting for a moment, would, to me, have been a thorough disappointment.

My visit to Mrs Akins was one of the most interesting events connected with the book. Another was the remark of David's senior partner, Arthur Lindsell, about my making the criminals in the dock say to themselves 'You don't understand, it's not as if anyone else had done it, with us it was different.' Mr Lindsell said that this was the characteristic reaction of the criminal: he thought I had done well to imagine it.

I had several suggestions, from English and American publishers, to write something else on the same lines. I would have found this, I am thankful to say, absolutely impossible. As I wrote to Victor Gollancz, you cannot do a thing like that except on a violent, spontaneous impulse of imagination. If it had been just possible, I might have been tempted to start on a course which would soon have worn out such imagination as I possessed. I am reminded of George Orwell's saying, that when people urge an author to write the same book again, they don't realise that if he could write it several times over, he couldn't have written it once.

My typing was done, for several years, in Hilda Brighten's office, called Brighten's Bureau. Its entry was half-way down Regent Street on your right; there was a lift but I always walked up the five flights to Hilda's office, on the top floor, under the roof. It consisted of two small rooms; the window of the business room looked down, down, into Regent Street, on to the tops of buses sliding far below. Hilda, stout and majestic, and to me always extremely kind, sat in the window while her assistant, Miss Albert, thin and despairing but a first-rate secretary, sat with her back to Mrs Brighten, typing madly.

Hilda had a fascinating background. Many of her connections were with the theatre, and it was an understood thing that you couldn't get anything lengthy done at short notice during the approach to Christmas as the Bureau was then fully occupied with typing pantomime scripts.

It was a superb establishment for any one who needed encouragement. Hilda read my work herself and if she liked it she would say in her deep hoarse voice when she put the typescript, neatly packed, into my hands: 'This is good.' Her opinion always proved an omen of success.

Hilda's father had been a wealthy entrepreneur who had, *inter alia,* financed the first fleet of taxi-cabs to work on the London streets. When he retired from the company, they gave him, as a badge, a gold taxi with jewels in the spokes of the wheels. He never forgave himself for passing-up the zip fastener: he had seen no future in it. Another of his rejections sounds more justifiable. An American firm with a base in Shaftesbury Avenue, selling patent medicines known as Munyon's Remedies, sent their representative to him with a case of samples. The case (which I saw) was exquisitely made, a rectangular box of polished wood, about twelve by eight inches, perhaps three inches deep. The lid was lined with ruched purple satin, the box itself lined with velvet, in which there were slots for glass tubes of which each tube was filled with a different sort of powder: these were remedies. The agent who offered them was a small, fair, inoffensive man; his name was Dr Hawley Harvey Crippen. When I saw the case, a few of the slots were empty – Hilda had once or twice taken out a tube to give to some favoured person. She said she knew she ought not to have done so, but nonetheless the relic was of great interest. She left it in her will to Madame Tussaud's.

Three

꠸

My father bought me a charming little house in Downshire Hill in 1939, just before the outbreak of war. I was to live in it continuously for fifty-five years until an accident which severely restricted my ability to walk forced me to move into a flat nearby in Hampstead.

Built in 1832, the house was one of a pair of the style that showed the last flicker of Regency architecture. Its narrow frontage had three sash-windows, one above the other, whose upper panes had glazing bars in Gothic arches. It was not convenient: it had only two rooms and a small landing on each floor – a large one in front and a smaller one behind – and a roomy double-basement, the front of which contained two generous cupboards, transformed by shelves into a larder and a pantry, but originally meant, as one saw by the fleur-de-lys-shaped airholes in the upper panels of each door, to accommodate truckle beds for servants. The kitchen range now enclosed a coke boiler. My father cut up the spacious, beautifully aspected top front room into a small sitting room, a bathroom and upstairs lavatory. One of the previous owners (who included Gordon Craig) had installed a bath on the top landing surrounded by a wooden horse-box, with the result that steam had reduced all the wallpapers on the top floor to hanging ribbons.

I had this beautiful but shabby eight-roomed house to myself, except that, in the early days, I occasionally let the first floor; and I had a constant stream of visitors, who much appreciated the opportunity to stay, given the shortage of hotel accommodation, during and immediately after the war. The premises were perfectly adequate for this, with my cooking and a series of remarkably kind 'helpers' on three days in the week; but with only one bathroom and one kitchen, they were not suitable for a long let.

The offices at which I worked during the war were all on the 24 bus route, so that on the return journey I often got off at Camden Town and walked up the Chalk Farm Road, passing a good many humble but active second-hand furniture shops which, owing to air raids and general disturbance of people's homes, were able to assemble a collection of chairs, tables, chests of drawers and looking-glasses such as I could never have afforded in normal conditions, and still less now, when the prices of antique furniture have rocketed. Over the six years of the war I was able, even with my small means, to do away with the Edwardian furniture from home with which I had originally furnished the house, and replace it with pieces of about the 1820–30 period. Even in those favourable circumstances, I could not have afforded the 1790–1820 range, but I had no unsatisfied longing when I saw how harmonious the interior of 8 Downshire Hill at last became. I had in all this much help from my mother; her standards were rigorous. It was not that she did not sympathise with my love of antique furniture: one of the most charming things I have, she gave me – a bow-fronted chest of drawers topped by a beautiful oval looking-glass on a little stand with drawers in it, which had belonged to her grandmother. But she felt that shabbiness was not to be tolerated even for the sake of elegance.

The only drawback to having this house to myself was that it made people who didn't know me assume that I was comfortably off, instead of being very hard up. I was constantly being asked by local people for subscriptions, which I found difficult to pay, even within the bounds of what must have looked like avarice and meanness. I was then approaching forty, but it gave me a retrospective indignation against people who harass students to part with their money. I remember reading an account by Margaret Drabble of how, in her youth, she had given a lecture to some association, for which the fee was five pounds, and how a woman had taken the money off her for some – no doubt worthy – cause before she left the building. Unless young novelists have an immediate monetary success, and very few of them do, they should not be asked, as they so frequently are, to give away copies of their books.

[41]

I still feel a certain resentment, largely against myself, over two cases of this sort. Two men whom I knew were, at different times, each staying with some moderately celebrated person (one was the wife of a previous prime minister). Both of them asked me to send him a copy of my current book, to give to the person with whom he was staying. I did this, and I never had a word of acknowledgement of either book: not from the people who had asked for them, or the people to whom, presumably, they were given.

It often takes me quite a long time to pick things up, but when I have done it, it is done. At a small party, the conversation turned on a book I had recently published, and one of the company, the son of a celebrated architect, said to me: 'Will you send me that?' I was astonished, but the general conversation swept on, without my having to answer. When I was leaving several people were seeing me off, and this young man joined them. Working his way to the front door, he said again: 'Will you send me that book?' This time I had to answer, but I did with a blank stare.

I will say here that if somebody wants to read a book, but doesn't want to buy it, they should either borrow it from somebody who has bought it, or ask for it at the nearest branch of their public library. If the library hasn't got it in already, it will do the author a good turn to have his or her name brought to their attention.

September 1939 was the date of my chance meeting in Hampstead with the property developer Erno Goldfinger. He seemed to have come to England much in advance of the German occupation of France, but while in Paris he had moved in the highest intellectual and aesthetic circles, and had the contempt for England and English society which you would, in the circumstances, expect. He was tall and cross-looking, and his manner, his admirers said, 'could be offensive'. From the one occasion in which I was in contact with him, I could endorse that opinion. In those days the Georgian Group was barely in existence, and the local council markedly Left, so Goldfinger had been allowed to tear down two Regency cottages in Willow Road, to replace them with a conception of his own. I met him briefly that September at a sherry party give by Amber Blanco White; the house occupied by her and her husband was on the side of Downshire Hill opposite to mine and the two houses were in view of each other. The street had then only one house of ugly modernity: all the rest were varied, enchanting gracefulness.

Goldfinger was saying goodbye to our hostess at the open front door, and I came up behind them at the tail of a conversation about air-raids. Goldfinger was saying, in his tone at once condescending and spiteful, 'All these houses are due to come down, anyway.' If I could, at that moment, have wreaked on him a severe personal injury, I believe I would have done it.

The National Trust has now acquired his house in Willow Road and opened it to the public. An issue of *N.W.3: The Magazine for Hampstead and Belsize Park* promises that we shall see the furniture Goldfinger designed for it, and some of the works of art he acquired. A photographic illustration shows a picture of a headless woman with flabby breasts and a horribly distended stomach; the other pictures in the photograph seem also to be of anatomical specimens but these are more difficult to identify. The caption says that these examples of the art Goldfinger collected over the years 'hang comfortably in his first floor dining room'.

You bet they do!

A most powerful counterpoise to Erno Goldfinger was another of my neighbours in Downshire Hill, a stout, valiant old lady, Miss Fanny Seeley. She was the daughter of Sir John Seeley, the Cambridge Professor of Modern History, author of *The Expansion of England*. She had been taught at home, some of her lessons by Sir John Seeley himself. When she told me this, I said: 'How wonderful to be taught history by *your* father!' and she said: 'Well, I don't know, he was always so much interested in *movements*. What I wanted to hear about was Queen Elizabeth's dresses.' I sympathised with her interest in Queen Elizabeth's dresses, but I could see that this attitude must have been rather a disappointment to Sir John Seeley. She could not, when I knew her, consider with interest anything of social history: welfare, medicine, education. All her enthusiasm was kept for her personal interests: the history and productions of the upper classes of the eighteenth and nineteenth centuries.

She owned a collection of the most desirable *objets*, from exquisite tables and chairs, to the travelling inkstand of Byron's physician, Dr Polidor, and a gold curl cut from the head of the dead Princess Charlotte. But in spite of, or even because of, this narrowness of her views, she was a tower of strength to us other householders in Downshire Hill. She led the successful struggle with Camden Council, who had intended to demolish the pair of houses immediately opposite mine, Nos 47 and 48, with sash-windows, fan-lights, and wrought-iron balconies, to make way for a block of council flats. The houses are still standing and are, of course, now recognised as too valuable to destroy. She was as vigilant in preserving the authentic traditions of the neighbourhood as she was in defending its architecture. She had heard that a pleasant, good-natured lady had bought one of the houses on the left side of the street, going towards the Heath, and was maintaining that his was the house to which Sarah Coleridge had come, to convalesce, taken care of by her friends. Miss Seeley had written to the lady, inviting her to submit her grounds for this assertion. The lady's reply, which Miss Seeley showed me, said that of course they didn't *know*, but they liked to *think* that it was under their pear-tree that Sarah Coleridge had lain in her chaise-longue. When I had read this, in a large sprawling hand on several sheets of lilac writing paper, Miss Seeley said what a pity it was to spread this sort of groundless tale, which hardened by repetition into a tradition, and she meant to write to the lady, saying so. I said rather faintly 'I'm afraid that will hurt her feelings.'

Until that moment I had never noticed the colour of Miss Seeley's eyes. I now saw that they were a very pale blue, which made the black pupils hard and sharp. She said: 'These matters are not a question of people's feelings, but of what can be *proved*.'

It was like seeing a ghost at midday.

The early days of September 1939 were passed in a sort of paralysis of apprehension, waiting for the terrific air-raids, which did not, in fact, come till the following year. For the autumn term of 1939 I went down to Royston once a week, where the headmistress Violet Hyett, with wonderful, practical skill, had transferred the King Alfred School; but she did not need me for flying visits and in any case a visit one day a week would not have seemed to the authorities a reason for my not being directed to war work. My chief impression of the early days was of the crowds of children who were being hurriedly removed from London, sometimes under the care of teachers or social workers, sometimes with their mothers who were being evacuated with them. Some of them took to the country joyfully, others, with their mothers, were so dissatisfied with it that they returned to London within twenty-four hours; but the majority of parents parted with their children, not happily but willingly, rather than risk their being mutilated, smothered or killed outright by houses crashing down on them in the nightmare of air-raids.

The one evacuee whom I personally met was a boy of twelve called Peter who was billeted on my aunt and uncle at Leatherhead. His father was the commissionaire of a London cinema and he was a fine example of a happy evacuee. My uncle's house was near watercress beds which for some reason attracted brilliant rainbows. One evening I stood at the front door, waiting for my uncle to take me to the station. Peter stood by me and we were entranced by a double rainbow: an outer one of pale hues, an inner one of vivid crimson, purple, blue and green. He said: 'When I'm a man, I'm going to live in the country.' I hope so much that he does.

With the outbreak of war, I was an obvious candidate for what was known as 'Directed Employment' and I was first assigned to a branch of the Assistance Board. This branch had been set up to help Jewish refugees, of whom there were so many that they swamped the regular Assistance Offices. It was first established in Alfred Place off Tottenham Court Road, but was soon transferred to one of the original buildings of Russell Square, whose front

[45]

windows overlooked the Square, while its doorway was just around the corner in Montague Place.

The interior of the house was of Regency date, almost intact, which was infuriating to the male clerks. The female ones were more tolerant, thinking only that it was 'a funny old place'; but to me it was endlessly interesting. The fact that the rooms had nothing in them now except office furniture – trestle tables, desks, filing cabinets – was far more satisfying than seeing them cluttered and obscured with modern furniture. The house, structurally, was almost exactly as Thackeray, in *Vanity Fair*, described that of the Osbornes in Russell Square, where the houses were built between 1800 and 1814; and as Thackeray described the Sedleys living there until about three years before Waterloo. He must have had the 1800 appearance of the houses in mind: 'the great, blank, stone staircases', 'the black marble dining room' on the ground floor (which was our Registry), 'the white marble chimneypiece' in the first floor drawing room. Thackeray says that behind the dining room was the room 'sacred to the master of the house, known as Mr Osborne's study'. This room looked out 'over a clean gravel court and to the stables'. The room behind the dining room and its window were still there, but outbuildings had concealed the stable-yard. However, when I once found myself on an errand in the office next door, there was the yard, outside the dining room window.

When John Lehmann commissioned me to write a preface to the Collins edition of *Vanity Fair*, published in 1954, I remembered the interior of 1 Montague Place as if I were still seeing it; I could stand in George Osborne's bedroom on the third floor, where Amelia, with young George beside her, stood looking over the trees of Russell Square to the house of her parents, 'where she had passed so many happy days of sacred youth'. I ended the preface saying 'It is sometimes used as a reproach to people that they "live in books", but "a good book is the precious lifeblood of a master-spirit", and we live more intensely when we have taken it into our own.'

When the Government had provided for the great tide of Jewish refugees, by support or finding them employment, they turned some of us over to the Assistance Board proper. As the first heavy air-raids over London began, stations were set up where the bombed-out victims could go to procure coupons for immediate necessities, such as clothes, bedding or tableware, and having been issued with them, could take them to one of several local depots where they exchanged them for whatever essentials they needed. A confidential note to Area Officers explained that though the Government accepted the fact that some of these claims might be spurious, since there was no time to investigate, they must be met immediately and without question, as one of the most important ways of avoiding general panic.

In 1 Montague Place a part of the hall behind the staircase had been sliced off to make a long slip-room with boarded walls. There was a bed in it, one of the ones we used when on fire-watching duty (the others were put up after closing time, among the tables, chairs and cabinets in the dining room). I was lying on this one, preparing to get up and start the morning tea-making, when the eight o'clock news began and I heard the announcement that Virginia Woolf had been found drowned in the River Ouse. It was said afterwards that she had dreaded another attack of mental derangement, from which she had felt sure that she would not recover. She had there-fore loaded her pockets with stones and drowned herself. A letter she had left for Leonard Woolf said: 'You have been so good.'

The mournful beauty of the story, against the background of 1941, was beyond words. None of my fellow office workers knew more of her than the name, many not even that. The chasm the news made in my consciousness was soon filled again, with chat, with conversation spasmodically very serious and the – to me – arduous office work, which I ought to have started at nineteen to have got the hang of properly. I owed a lot to the friendliness and good nature of the other staff: the men, particularly, did their best to shove me along. When some work came before us, such as alter-ing the date on 500 forms from 1939 to 1941, they would say in tones of hearty self-congratulation: 'Here's something Little Betsy can do!'

I knew, instinctively, that my colleagues would be repelled by my aesthetic delight in Montague Place, so I concealed it as well as I could; but when I could get about, unnoticed, in an early or a late lunch hour, I would steal into vacated rooms. The most spectacular was the first floor drawing room, divided by folding doors; the front half had French windows opening on to a balcony protected by wrought-iron railings. From this room the chimneypiece had disappeared (probably ripped away and sold), but when I had an opportunity to go into the office next door, I saw what it had been like. Only the ground floor here was in occupation as offices, so I was able to go quietly up to the first floor. In the dusk of a winter afternoon, amongst darkened walls, across the distance of an empty boarded floor, a white marble chimneypiece, wreathed and garlanded, stood out in ethereal distinctness. Perhaps it looked more striking than it did when newly carved and polished, astride a blazing fire with brass ornaments, surrounded by velvet and chintz.

After one of the early raids on London, in a street in Bloomsbury I came upon a little heap of broken china on a pavement, relics of pieces of Sunderland ware, parts of a sugar basin and cream jug, all in pieces, hopelessly beyond repair; sections of the black etching of trees in a park were visible on the fragments, and on some you could see the rim, with the mottled, rosy-lilac lustre. These remains had been reduced to utter uselessness, and yet I picked them up and carried them home; I kept them till I had, happily, collected china of the same period, intact.

Meantime, as the first and third of my postings were in Montague Place and Store Street, I used to spend part of my lunch-breaks walking up and down the streets of Tottenham Court Road, which otherwise I would never have visited on foot. One day I was riveted outside a bookseller's window in Museum Street. I was fond of Susan Ferrier's novel *Inheritance*, published in 1824, in which Gertrude, the young Countess of Rossville, is embarrassed by a call from her vulgar Cockney relations, who roam about her drawing room, examining books and engravings. Mrs Larkins exclaims: 'This is beautiful! I never saw this before: Fish, by Mrs Tigg.'...

'Dear! Is that Fishy!' said Miss Larkins, 'Sweet, purty thing it is!' Gertrude could have wept at this rendering of 'Psyche, by Mrs Tighe'. I had never heard of the work, outside the pages of *Inheritance*, and was charmed to see, opened to display in the bookseller's window, the frontispiece of a kneeling figure in Regency Classical dress, opposite the title-page 'Psyche, by Mrs Tighe, 1805'.

But in those times, getting one's midday meal was an even more serious matter than roaming about. I was fortunate that two out of three of my offices were in easy walking distance of Heal's furniture shop which then included a restaurant. As the company had always been vegetarian, this had a standing repertoire of excellent meatless dishes. The management were past masters of pure, rich vegetable soups, large, hot floury baked potatoes (a course in themselves), spaghetti loaded with mushrooms (instead of sparsely strewn in them), while their puddings were delicious: they included frumenty, an old English dish, of which I had often read but never tasted till then – it was made of roasted cereals, sprinkled with raisins, and eaten with cream (the latter was, in wartime ,artificial, but one adjusted to it).

The restaurant had a large, regular clientele and excellent, elderly waitresses; but one or two of these had disappeared and been replaced by younger ones of a very different sort. A client of long standing, when one of these slapped his bill in front of him, said: 'You haven't brought me my coffee.' 'You didn't order it.' 'Yes I did, at the time I ordered my lunch.' 'Well, you should have said again, when I brought your sweet.' 'I thought you'd remember it,' he said pleasantly. 'Oh no,' she said. 'Nothing of that sort *now*.' This sort of ill-will was apt to erupt from people who felt that it was now *their* turn. Women engaged to serve at the counters of shops in Oxford Street would be seen standing in their outdoor clothes twenty minutes before closing-time. At one of these shops I was buying a collar, choosing from among half a dozen. I asked the witchlike character behind the counter the price of the one I wanted. She answered shrewishly: 'I've told you once already.' But the most telling rebuff I received was in the canteen which the

Assistance Board shared with other offices. It was a large hall with trestle tables across it, from which the plates of the first course were cleared away by the roughest women one had ever seen. One day I was sitting at the corner of one of the tables, listening to the general conversation, when the woman employed to clear found that my chair was a little too far out as she turned the corner, and gave the rung a savage kick which drove my ribs into the table's edge. These experiences, however, tended to make one more grateful and appreciative of the kindness and cheerful good will of the local shop-keepers, the postmen, policemen, bus conductors, railwaymen, to say nothing of street-sweepers, coalmen, dustmen, those invaluable helpers who kept other people's daily lives going.

Our office was one of those where clerks were given brief instructions as to how to cope with the applicants and, having been instructed, were rushed around to different areas, wherever there had been a raid the night before, not knowing, until their arrival at the office in the morning, in what area their work was to be. When we arrived the injured and the dying had been borne away to hospitals, but we were faced with people who had endured the most terrifying experiences. Their windows shattered, their roofs blown off, their walls shaken to pieces. Some of them had piles of brick and board tumbling down on them or had been lifted out of cavities into which fallen beams had pinned them, but were able to walk and to say what had happened to them, though sometimes still powdered with the dust from the plaster. They displayed extraordinary courage; most of them spoke cheerfully though some were gruff with dismay. I remember, however, one young woman who had not been physically injured but was deadly pale and unable to speak. She was accompanied by her brother-in-law who gently repeated our brief questions to her, but she was in such a state of shock she could not utter a word. He filled in her declaration for her and took her away on his arm. A sight that did one's heart good was that of an elderly man in pyjamas and dressing-gown, blood-stained bandage round his head, and a bowler hat poised smartly on top of it.

In different streets, in many parts of London, one might see houses with façades blown off, exposing their storeys with a looking-glass, a picture, a lavatory cistern, visible on the remaining walls. The nearest I came to a scene of utter destruction was walking down Gower Street to the Ministry of Information, in the last phase of an air-attack. All down Gower Street were doors hanging crooked in front of flaming interiors, while roadsweepers were piling glass fragments into shimmering heaps at the edges of the pavements.

I cannot cease to be thankful that I never experienced the extreme horrors of air-raids. The houses in Downshire Hill were so fragile that when a bomb dropped on the Heath, the walls shook and plaster dropped from the cornices of the ceiling; but one reads of a midwife who crawled into a drainpipe to deliver a woman who had sought shelter there in the final throes of labour, and of a woman who, with a child in her arms of under two years old, had taken refuge in a concrete shelter which had collapsed on top of her.

'I was screaming, the baby was screaming, I tried to ease myself away so that the baby could breathe, because everything was crushing us... it seemed ages but I think it was only a few minutes when I heard movements and voices about me and I'm saying: "Please help me, please help me." Gradually, I managed to put my arm out, and somebody was holding my hand and saying: "Hold on, lady, hold on!" and I said, "I've got a baby, got a baby in my arms", and they pulled my baby out and got me out.' (*London at War*, p. 130.)

In spite of people who had suffered terror, mutilation or death, it was wonderful how much of ordinary life went on, adapted to wartime conditions. Some of the routine of the Assessment Department involved the searching out of applicants' files. These lay in piles on side-tables and window-sills; if they had been in use some time the coloured cover had developed a dingy, rubbed, almost furry surface. Their registry number was inked on the cover and sometimes one had to look really hard to relate the number on one's list for which one was searching with these large, but now strangely illegible, figures on the file cover.

It does not sound very taxing work, nor was it, compared with cryptography or munition-making, but it could be, strangely enough, extremely tiring, reducing one almost to despair, searching through piles, sometimes thirty or forty high, of cardboard-covered files and trying to identify on the flimsy, carbon-paper contents with the information for which one was searching. There was, however, one among us who was so rapid and expert that sometimes a message would come from the head of a room: 'Tell Miss Sapstead to drop everything and find me file number so-and-so.' Pussy Sapstead was not pretty, but exceptionally attractive, all curves, with curly hair and round, rolling dark eyes. Her ankles were so slender that they, and high-heeled shoes, made her feet almost like hooves. She was unfailingly cheerful and self-confident, and welcomed by the men wherever she went; but she could not stay long with any of them: either some authority required her services immediately, or some lucky chap was waiting for her impatiently. One morning quite a serious conversation on Feminism had broken out. There weren't any men present, and the consensus of opinion was that women, as a whole, were treated with shameless exploitation and basic injustice. Pussy Sapstead had been visiting our window-sills on one of her Class A file-finding missions and had been, as usual, successful. She now paused in the open doorway, with a collection of files poised on her hip, and made her contribution. 'Oh well,' she said, 'we've always had a nice time and I dare say we always shall', before disappearing from our sight.

I think of her and I remember Germaine Greer's statement in her book *The Female Eunuch*: 'Women have no idea how much men hate them.' Pussy Sapstead hadn't: not the slightest.

Towards the end of 1941, the Assistance Board closed down our part of the office and directed members elsewhere. I found myself in the Board of Trade. A large part of this ministry was lodged in the then newly-built flats, Dolphin Square, on the brink of the Thames below Westminster. Each block was called after a naval celebrity. We were in Raleigh, a department dealing with clothing and textile coupons. At the head of the room in which I was at first was a young man whom the armed forces had not found strong enough for active service; but he was very bright, and had naturally been put in charge. He was like a very clever schoolboy, intelligent but completely without experience of the world. We received a letter from the head of a police station asking for supplementary clothing coupons. He explained that he had to rely on untrained men without police experience, and the full police uniform would be a help to them in their task of keeping order. Our young friend wrote, as he was obliged to do, that the Board could not meet this request, but he added, out of his own head, surely a policeman's authority should rest in himself, not in his uniform? This brought us a letter from the Chief Constable.

Of the many individual cases which we were called on to handle, one which stays in my mind was an urgent request for a complete clothing supplement from a miner who had been in a pit accident. The form was correctly filled in, but tucked into it was a small page of lined paper, obviously torn out of a notebook. On it was written: 'When they took me out of the pit, they only gave me my boots back. Yours sincerely, Mr G. Stokes.' I rushed into the appropriate department and laid the form and its attachment before the official in charge. He agreed that it must go off at once; so instead of remaining in the bottom of his in-tray till it worked itself to the top, it was sent off to Mr G. Stokes by that morning's midday post.

The work of the department brought me into telephone contact with physicians, surgeons and the matrons of hospitals. I cannot vouch for the entire accuracy of this, but the current story was that when rationing of medical clothing was under discussion, the Royal College of Surgeons sent a deputation to the Board, laying down the quantity of coupon-free garments they absolutely required. The Board said: 'Of course we understand your needs are a number one priority, but if you are to have all this, coupon-free, we shan't be able to do anything for the physicians: they will have to come out of the Concession altogether.' The surgeons said that was unfortunate, but it couldn't be helped. So from that time till the end of the rationing period, after the war, you had the laughable situation that the physicians had to tip up coupons for white coats and for aprons, while the surgeons, most of whose work was done in operation theatres, got every shred of clothing for it coupon-free, as it was called 'impersonal issue'.

Some hospital matrons were in almost desperate plight; their nurses when on duty were required to wear black stockings which, out of uniform, they would never put on, and they bitterly resented having to give up coupons for them. The Concession covered all the rest of the uniform, but matrons were sometimes faced by student nurses who resigned to go and make munitions, where they could keep all their coupons to themselves. Therefore, being by nature and training somewhat formidable, and feeling that they must fight it *à l'outrance*, the matrons naturally took it out on whoever answered them on the telephone.

When this was I, they would have a walkover, except that it was impossible to go behind the Board's ruling on the matter; and it was the Board's system that the persons who dealt with inquiries were not the ones who had any say in the making of the policies.

One morning I was answering a call from the matron of a hospital, and repeating weakly 'I am very sorry, I really am, but I'm afraid that's what the Board does say' and she rang off with a high, bitter laugh. As I put back the receiver, I found I had been overheard by a pleasant, elderly man, the head of another department, who had been on his way elsewhere and had paused to listen to my grovelling performance. He said, 'I am not finding fault, but if that had been *my* call, I should have said: "Frankly, Matron, the Board already gives you a most generous concession." I thought: 'My word! That's the way! I *will* say that, next time.' Next time, naturally, wasn't very long coming. When I took the call from yet another powerful but distracted lady, I said, with what I had hoped was dignified reserve, 'Can I help you?' It was a matter of seconds before I was back: 'I am *very* sorry, matron, but I am afraid we can't do anything: that is what the Board does say.'

These bruising occasions perhaps led me on to a piece of somewhat unprofessional conduct. Some time after this, a call was put through from a surgeon whose name was well known. He asked me two questions, both of which I had to tell him I couldn't answer, as he was talking to the wrong department. At the second one, he said: 'You seem to be a very ignorant little girl!' I repeated, in desperation, 'I'm sorry, but you've got the wrong department. If you will get back to the switchboard and tell them...' He uttered an imprecation, and feeling that I must recoup myself, I said: 'But would you be interested in a pair of coupon-free rubber gloves?' He exclaimed: 'Try me!' I said: 'They are not on issue at this moment, but if you apply' (and I told him where to do this) 'you will be sure to get a pair, because your name will be very high on the list.' He summoned, I suppose, his secretary, and made me repeat the address for her to write down. Then, with a belated sense of caution, I said: 'Don't tell anybody I told you, will you?' He said: 'Of course not, my dear!' and you could almost hear him purring at the other end of the line.

In Raleigh I was fortunate in having a desk immediately beside a large window, directly overlooking the Thames, screened by plane trees with delicate branches that tasselled the air with their leaves. At one moment, one second even, just after 9.30 a.m., the sunrise struck the river and the whole breadth of it, behind the plane trees, turned to glittering crimson; then, within seconds, it became bright silver, quivering behind the trees. I used to watch for this phenomenon; it happened, morning after morning, for perhaps a week. There was no one to whom to point it out, and if there had been, there would have been no time to fetch them before it vanished.

The room behind the office where I sat was occupied by several women clerks who sat together at a big table. They were middle-aged, broad and solid, and their voices were heavy and harsh. I had occasionally to give them a message, or ask for something they could supply. I am sure my manner was not offensive – it is not, I hope, by nature – and becoming very early aware of their dislike, I was particularly careful not to give offence; but I was always received with as much resentment as if I had gone out of my way to affront them. However hard I tried, do what I would, I was unfor-givable. I had become resigned to going in and out with the mini-mum of words that my business required, uttered with perhaps exaggerated courtesy. Then I received a remarkable insight. A girl who ran errands, pretty, slender, much made-up and brightly dressed, was standing by the main table, quietly whimpering, sniff-ing and dabbing her eyes. The elderly women found out the cause of her grief: someone who had arranged to meet her hadn't turned up. Their exclamations showed both that they thought it too bad, but that they urged her not to take on about it. They were so warm-hearted and encouraging, so sensible, both sympathising with her and gently laughing at her; it was unforgettable.

I left the Board of Trade in 1943, having been accepted as a clerk in the Ministry of Information for what was to prove the last two years of the war. I owed this appointment to the influence of Eliza-beth Bowen who knew everybody and to whose recommendations everybody listened; her kindness to me was unfailing.

The premises the Ministry then occupied were a part of the University of London, at the bottom of Store Street. By great good fortune my friend Ann Sitwell was also employed there, in the department known as the Far East. The presiding genius here was Mr Arthur Waley, whose translation of the novel of Japanese court life, *The Tale of Genji*, was by then world-famous. It never ceased to surprise one that though this work's atmosphere – the elegant simplicity of extreme sophistication – reminded one of Proust, it had, in fact, been written in the era when the English were under-going the roughness and barbarity of the Norman Conquest.

Mr Waley was very tall and thin and carried an air of supreme intellectual and social superiority. It was said that his peculiar into-nation, high, thin, expressionless and dismal, was the result of his intensive Japanese studies; these may or may not have caused him to intone as the Japanese do: at all events they, or some other causes, had prevented him from speaking like an ordinary English person, but he was formidable. In the room which was his main office, he sat the head of a very long table, clerks down each side of it, and a telephone at his elbow. One must admit that Ann probably had more calls 'put through' to her than any head of department would think reasonable. Mr Waley in fact became somewhat rasped and when a voice on the telephone asked if Miss Sitwell was there, he would say 'No' in his outlandish key, though Ann was sitting a couple of yards away from him. However, one day he met his match. Ann really was out of the room when a young naval officer, on a brief spell of leave, asked if she were there, and when he received the usual 'No', he said: 'Then take a message for her, will you, there's a good chap. Got pencil and paper handy? Right, then – this is so-and-so speaking', and he dictated the place and the time of the rendezvous. When Ann came back, Mr Waley speechlessly put the paper in front of her. The telephone conversation had been audible to the people on each side of Mr Waley, so she got the benefit of that too.

Another significant figure was in a nearby office; this was Mr Lyle, who used to speak of himself as 'poor old Tommy Lyle', though one could not see why, as he seemed (although not of course the equal in puissance of Mr Waley) to be well-established and highly thought of. He was sympathetic and knowledgeable about all the great religions, and had a fund of interesting stories about the eminent theosophist, Madame Blavatsky. He had brought from his flat a Japanese screen, covered in its original cotton, fragile and battered but extensive, and this he had arranged across the front of his desk; and at the same time he had fastened a little tinkling bell on his door which sounded every time the door was pushed open, so giving him a few seconds' warning to leave off meditation and reconnect himself with the official world.

One day, during his lunch hour, he discovered in a local shop a censer, part of the strange flotsam and jetsam of the time; it can't, I suppose, have been silver, but it polished up as if it were. The bowl was elaborately chased; three chains were fastened to its rim and united in a ring above it. I brought in metal polish and cloths and spent part of several lunch hours polishing and repolishing; it was laborious, but the finished result was brilliant. Mr Lyle was delighted. 'But now', he said, with a speculative look, 'we need incense.' We did not know where to go for this, but he suggested Burns, Oates and Washbourne, the well-known Catholic suppliers near Victoria Station. Ann, who was then living in that direction, hied off to it on her way home and came back next morning with a packet of rose incense. In the lunch hour Mr Lyle ignited the incense and swung the censer. I had smelt the perfume before, but never from a censer at close quarters. The scent was ravishing – hot, pungent, stimulating, giving one indescribable emotion. It filled the room and wafted out into the corridor. Mr Lyle said it would soon dissipate, and he went to his office, carrying the censer with him. Sure enough, the scent faded from my room till it was only a heavenly breath. What we had not bargained for was that as it left our floor level, it rose to the one above, where two elderly ladies were occupied. They came out into the corridor in a paroxysm of indignation, exclaiming that they would complain to the Director General, and invoking the Protestant Truth Society (founded, we afterwards discovered, in 1859, ' to fight the growing influence of Romanism and Liberalism in the Church'). Mr Lyle, calling himself now with some reason 'poor old Tommy Lyle', told us all this, and how he apologised to the ladies, explaining that he had only tried a little experiment with a new purchase, admitting that he ought to have waited to do this till he got home. One of the ladies said, somewhat suspiciously, 'All right, so long as there isn't any more of it.' The other one turned her back on him, not trusting herself to speak.

Meantime I had been placed as an assistant to Theodora Benson, who enlarged the scope of my perceptions very much. She was tall and very slight, and would have been altogether lovely if she had not always looked on the verge of severe illness. She had belonged to débutante society; and though much of its luxury and amusement had been stripped away by wartime conditions, the framework remained. Her close friend Betty Askwith was also in a department of the Ministry. They had done the social round together and each published amateurish but charming novels. They had a wide circle of friends and perpetual engagements though did not seem to enjoy these very much: the latter seemed to be in the region of duty rather than pleasure. Betty made a very happy marriage with Keith Miller Jones, a solicitor, whom she described as 'as tall as Mr Darcy, but much sweeter-tempered'. Theodora's vital energies seemed to be exercised in encouraging and befriending. Her sister, Antonia, was married to Lord Radcliffe, who later chaired the committee which arranged the boundary between India and Pakistan, but was now the Director General of the Ministry of Information.

The department of which Theodora was the most effective and important member was 'Speaker's Notes'. These were pamphlets with brief, simple explanations of Government policy, which appeared to be largely centred on rationing, but also covered other policies for the use of speakers appointed to address public audiences. The Notes gave the foundation, but it was open to speakers to adapt or enlarge them, according to what was likely to interest a particular audience.

My work was, at first, to consult newspaper files and current publications, by which Theodora checked her Notes. She had had, just before the war, a brilliant, brief career in popular journalism, like the flash of a kingfisher across a stream, and her style, for the medium, was perfect. When the material was assembled, she put it together in exactly the way best suited to catch public attention and to explain the reasons for public policy in a way that was both reliable and vivid.

I do not remember how it came about that Theodora relinquished this department for another, but I now became assistant to her successor, Rohan Butler, a man much younger than I was, who had already enjoyed a distinguished opening to his career. He was a Fellow of All Souls, and had published a book, profound yet eminently readable, *The Roots of Nazi Philosophy*. His conversation was endlessly interesting, he knew so much that I wanted to know, he was so unfailingly kind and charming, the hours spent in the office often did not seem like work. One major benefit he bestowed on me was that he introduced me to A. L. Rowse who was to give me invaluable inspiration and help when, later on, I published my book about Queen Elizabeth, *Elizabeth the Great*.

I was next promoted from assembling the material for Speaker's Notes to being one of the note writers, which meant that what I wrote had to be submitted to Rohan for his approval, in the course of which I learned from him a good deal of what should be said, and still more of what should not be said, when you speak in public. One day when I had been obliged to alter and rearrange several times, I exclaimed, 'Theodora was so much better at this that I am.' He said: 'She was better than any of us.'

Rohan had been transferred, on the outbreak of the war, from the Foreign Office to the Ministry of Information, and his chief work here was to bring out, every week, the War Commentary for publication in *The Times* on Friday mornings. This meant assimilating and arranging a conspectus of all the war news, in every theatre, published during the past week, which required from him a thorough grasp of the action, of all the services on all fronts. The only part I played in this, apart from some routine searching, was to fetch reports from the military department. The news could be collected only at the last possible moment on Thursday evening so that it was not out of date in the next morning's *Times*. I had to ask for their reports from some impatient and severe officers who were sitting over them, no doubt with nerves considerably tried. A long stone staircase separated their floors from ours below, and I remember hovering up and down it in a state bordering on panic: the military had said the news material was not ready, and when I returned to Rohan with these tidings, he said 'Go back and tell them I've got to have it.' I stole up the stairs as slowly as I could, to lengthen the time since they saw me last, but when I presented myself again they didn't give me a chance to say anything: one of them exclaimed in tones of harshness I had never heard used to me before, 'I've already told you, madam, that material isn't ready!'

When I got back to our office, I suppose I looked so distraught at my appearing empty-handed that I didn't need to say what my reception had been. Rohan took up the telephone and in a tone of gentlemanly firmness asked if he could have the material within half an hour. After the reply, his thanks were so cordial and friendly, so casual even, that he had obviously done something possible only for the head of a department. He set the seal on his exploit by going upstairs for the papers himself.

It was a feature of the wartime newspapers that whatever topic emerged, so dramatic that it was front-page news in the dailies, it was immediately succeeded by another of equal urgency and reduced to small print or wiped off the page altogether. One episode remained vividly with me.

During the second period of intensive air-raids, a new wave of children were evacuated, among them two brothers aged twelve and nine, who were sent to a farm on the borders of Herefordshire. An investigation clerk aged nineteen, in her first post, was sent on a routine visit to the children to make sure that all was well with them. (This post of investigating clerk was one I had held in my appointment at the Assistance Board.) When she interviewed the boys she was made uneasy by an impression she could not define; she took them out into the fields where they could not be overhead, and said 'Now, are you all right?' But she was defeated by that reaction (well-known to the police) that suffering children sometimes display, of refusing to tell a stranger what is the matter. They replied: 'Yes we're all right.' She could only go back to her office, but there she wrote a report of her visit, saying that for some reason she could not explain she felt seriously uneasy about the boys' condition, and adding: 'I recommend immediate investigation.' The office did nothing. Nine days later, the younger boy was found dead, manslaughtered by the farmer.

Then the balloon went up. An inquest on the dead child was followed by the trial of the farmer and his wife, which resulted in a term of imprisonment for both of them. The girl, had she been more experienced, when she found her recommendation ignored would have said to be head of the department: 'You've had my report recommending immediate investigation; if you haven't acted on it in twenty-four hours' time, I shall take the matter to the police.' But at nineteen and in her first post she was the person least to blame in the matter. As to who were to blame, the public were in no doubt at all. Some members of the local council were obliged to appear as witnesses, and they much resented the manner in which the court addressed them. One of them was a stout, elderly, domineering lady with an elaborate coiffure of grey hair. She was obliged, however grudgingly, to answer the coroner, but she absolutely refused to speak to the journalists who thronged the exit of the court. As soon as the witnesses were let loose, they hurried to the railway station pursued by journalists whose blood was up now. The train was already waiting. The elderly lady scuttled down the platform towards it, chased by journalists yelling at her. It was wrong, but it gave one some satisfaction to read it.

Agatha Christie made a radio play out of this material, calling it *The Mousetrap*. This was listened to with absorbed interest by Queen Mary, who said: 'I think Miss Christie should make a stage play of it.' This, it is said, was the origin of the world's longest-running theatrical feature to date. I do not know how many modifications it may have gone through over the years; when I saw it, not long after its opening, the likeness of the stout elderly lady with the elaborate grey coiffure was still intact.

Four

8

I have never been a distinguished cook – unlike my brother Romilly's wife, who was off to a flying start as her mother was a Frenchwoman. Céline not only produces delicious dishes from recipes outside one's ken; she has the fine cook's inability to give you, off-hand, the weights and measures and the oven-times for what she does by instinct. If you say 'How much flour?' her answer is 'Oh, just enough.' 'How long should you have it in the oven?' 'Just till it's done.' When the details are absolutely demanded of her, she can of course produce them, but I think she has never asked the questions of herself.

In the time immediately after the war, although I was spending a great deal of energy writing, I did concentrate on improving myself as a cook. There were not then those excellent articles on cookery that you now find in the Sunday papers, but good ones were scattered here and there, and I collected recipes from people I knew. I found that tinned tomato soup, which I have always disliked, can be made delicious by adding to it orange juice and the liquid out of a can of tinned pimentos; that shepherd's pie is transformed if you mix a tablespoon of Bovril with the mince before putting on the potato roof. One dish for which I collected the recipe requires a deep china basin (which fortunately I had) in which you mix joints and pieces of roast chicken, grilled mushrooms and slices of hard-boiled egg; you then pour aspic over them up the bowl's rim. When set this makes an excellent compound; you cannot serve any potatoes with it, as their heat makes the aspic run, but the dish is so substantial, the head of an Iceberg lettuce or Little Gem is all it needs.

An item which I found in a woman's paper was how to make a very successful sorbet with Ribena currant juice, stiffly beaten whites of egg and, when firm, coated on top with double cream. It so happened that no one to whom I offered it had tasted it before, so it enjoyed a *succès d'estime*. However, I cannot remember where I found the most original recipe I used. You made, in a saucepan, a strong brew of China tea and soaked prunes in it overnight. Next morning, having strained it, you stewed the prunes in it gently; when they were cold, you extracted the stones, cracked them and took out the little almond-tasting kernels; with the prune-flavour China tea, you made a loose jelly, into which you returned the prunes, scattering the little kernels over them. The result was *recherché*, but it took rather a long time to compose, so I did not make it very often.

My dinner parties could never be for more than six, including me. The dining room was the smaller of the ground floor rooms; it was square, and I had been able to buy, from someone who didn't want it, rather a large George IV round mahogany table on a triangular base, which, with six dining room chairs of the same type, filled the room except for a narrow slip of a sideboard; so I acquired (for £3 off the pavement in Hampstead High Street) a more suitable 'pier table' with a white marble top and gilt legs. It was in very shabby condition when I bought it, but when scrubbed down and regilded it was just what the room needed. The small square carpet was scarlet, and the walls painted dead white.

As I had a white Leeds dessert service, I tried to have everything on the dinner table white. I had six goblets in milk glass; red wine or rosé looked beautiful in them, but they did not suit anything else. From a hardware shop I bought six ordinary tumblers and a water-jug of the same type; the shopkeeper 'knew of someone' who would paint the jug and glasses all over with spots of glossy white paint, finishing them off with a scalloped white edge round the rims. In varying lights, the spots looked like a snowstorm. All broken now, long since!

At the end of the war, Romilly was released from the Foreign Office and returned to Cambridge, but he made frequent visits to

Downshire Hill and he put me right on one important point. I used to think that inferior sherry didn't matter, but wine should be as good as one could afford. This, I learned, was the wrong way about: sherry should be the best you could buy (not very taxing, as I didn't drink myself, and it kept indefinitely). Wine, he said, should be as good as you can compass, but no need to break your heart over it. 'Look at the French,' he said 'that's how *they* do it.' He meant, of course, the French of slender means such as mine.

Over the years I increased the standard of heating in the house. All the rooms had beautiful grates for open fires, but some time after the war I heard that the firm of Pither could supply and fit stoves of various periods. I got from them one of 1830, with the metal frame moulded in pointed arches like my window panes. When it was in place, they told me exactly the right sort of coke to order, and old as it was, the stove functioned splendidly, warming the ground floor, and when the light was turned off, filling the drawing room with a deep red-gold glow.

I still liked to collect wood for my bedroom and the rooms of guests who might prefer a wood fire to an electric radiator to go to bed. The strip of wooded green at the bottom of Keats Grove was a particular hunting ground. There were plane trees too, at intervals down Rosslyn Hill and as I got my eye in, I found more and more nuggets of burnable wood strewn about, consisting largely of the thickened areas where the twigs had joined the branches. I stopped to collect them and put them in my shopping basket, regardless of the surprise of passers-by.

My most exacting guest of this era, who caused me the greatest nervous agitation, was Dr R. W. Chapman. The popular cult of Jane Austen has expanded so rapidly of late years that the wide audience whose knowledge of the novels is confined to television versions of *Pride and Prejudice, Sense and Sensibility* and *Emma* would not understand how awful a figure Dr Chapman was to us in the 1940s. Deirdre Le Faye and Brian Southam have carried on and upheld the tradition of scholarly examination of Jane

Austen's family records, her childhood writings and her letters, but Dr Chapman was the first authority of high scholarship to undertake the project and his beautiful edition of novels and letters, issued by the Clarendon Press in 1923, accompanied by notes and biographical details, and illustrated by enchanting contemporary prints and engravings, has paved the way for all succeeding ones. It so happened that he had known Theodora Benson's mother, Lady Charnwood (who had held him in high esteem). After the war when hotel accommodation was extremely scarce and Dr Chapman wanted to come to London rather often, he used the family connection to gain himself a perch in the flat high up over Piccadilly which Theodora then inhabited. She was sweetness and good nature itself but she was not very much interested in Jane Austen, and rather glad to be able to shift the cares of entertaining him on to me, believing I would be charmed to undertake them.

He was very tall, very thin and rather cross, but he was not difficult to entertain; all he wanted was warmth and quiet during the day, with his meals brought to him, and in the evening, a little cheerful, carefully selected worthwhile company. On his first visit he said his only out of the way requirement was tea at 5.30 in the morning. Might he go down to the kitchen and make it for himself? I hurriedly procured an electric kettle and arranged a tea-tray for him last thing at night. As his room was over my bedroom I used to wake up to the brief whistle of the kettle very early in the morning. It reminded me of the mysterious whistle which Helen Stonor heard in the early hours in Conan Doyle's *The Adventure of the Speckled Band*.

Dr Chapman became particularly fond of my closest female friend at the time, Ann Sitwell. I find it impossible to give any adequate idea of her. She married three times and had innumerable passing love-affairs, including one devastating one, for which I felt particularly concerned, as I had introduced the man to her. Every man I ever heard speak of her, all, in their differing idioms, said how extraordinarily attractive they found her. She was indeed very pretty, with a Cupid's bow mouth; her figure was slender with a full bosom; her sympathy was deep and immediately called out; but none of this conveys her charm. In what does overpowering sexual attractiveness consist? But more important to ask, perhaps, is what comes of it? Judging by the one case I knew well, and the few others I have seen at a distance, one would say that in the long run, too much of it is as fatal to happiness as too little. She garnered plenty of pleasure and excitement, but so much pain, it is dreadful to remember. Besides this extraordinary power, she was also highly educated; she could talk, and listen to an academic man, whatever the subject. Though Dr Chapman appreciated the conveniences of Downshire Hill, its attraction for him was, as I had seen, that on their first meeting she had captivated him, and that she thoroughly enjoyed his conversation and, in spite of his age, his homage. I always, afterwards, asked her to come when he was there. There was nothing in this 'out of line' as soldiers say; it was just a sort of earthly paradise. Her attitude to him was one of admiration, affection and respect. To him, she was like Persephone, walking through the flowery meadow, gathering flowers, in the vale of Enna – I was more than happy to leave the conversation to her, while I got on with various household matters.

In what turned out to be his last letter to me (I think he was feeling himself too old to come to London any more) he said: 'Your affection has meant a great deal to me.' This was unexpected, though he had once addressed us as 'You two, blest pair of sirens.'

Dr and Mrs Murray Baker, my neighbours for twenty years, occupied No. 7, the house to which mine was attached. The date of the pair being 1832, an era of graceful but rapidly run-up buildings, their walls were fragile. If either household had been in any way unneighbourly, the other would have suffered keenly. As it was, there was just a pleasant consciousness of life near at hand. One result of this neighbourhood was that my house was proved to be cat-friendly. All the time of their occupation of No. 7, the Murray

Bakers, besides raising a fine family of two boys and two girls, supported a series of Siamese cats. The last in the succession, and the longest-lived, came, I believe, to look upon No. 8 merely as an extension of No. 7. My first sight of him was on a morning when I opened my front door and found a tiny Siamese kitten on the step, looking up at me with his blue eyes. I telephoned Mrs Baker and she came round to fetch him, asking me if I would do anything I could to prevent his going out on to the road. I undertook this eagerly but she herself had a remarkable influence on her cats which restrained them from going out on to the hill; and with two front gardens and two back ones, side by side, they had no pressing need to roam.

All the cats, and particularly the last, whose name was Cad, were magnetised towards my house, in a way that delighted me. For a short time the Bakers' daughter, Jane, came to stay with her parents and brought a large, superb white cat, whose name, in fact, was Sam, but I called him 'White' merely, and my helper, Mrs Hollis, 'Old White', which gave him a sort of folklore dignity and significance. There had been a small wooden shed in my back garden, in a corner outside the dining room window and the party fence. As the householders of Downshire Hill were engaged in a perpetual warfare against damp, my builder advised me to remove the shed from contact with the house, so it was re-established further up the garden path. While it was in its original position, however, its roof afforded White a convenient take-off to the sill of my first-floor back bedroom. He formed an extraordinary attachment to this site; I always left doors open in the daytime, and whenever, during this era, I went upstairs to the first landing, I would look into the back bedroom, and, as often as not, a glance would show me White's noble back view as he perched on the outer sill, looking out pensively over the garden.

No. 7 was a quarter as big again as my house. My front door was in a side wall, but at No. 7 there was an extension of the façade which framed the front door and opened into a spacious hall (whereas mine was only a few feet square). Above the Bakers' hall was a small room with its own gothic window, overlooking Downshire Hill. Their front garden was overshadowed by a magnificent weeping ash, whose delicate but vigorous sprays sprang up like a fountain, then, curving and drooping down, made almost a tent. When the foliage was fully out and all the surrounding bushes and hedges in their deepest green, the dim but transparent effect of greenery as you went up to the Bakers' front door was lovely. Betty Baker had green fingers. Her spring flowers only gave way to summer ones; her white roses were exquisite, and she had flowering shrubs I cannot name.

My garden, though immediately next door, had an arid soil. I had had the beds dressed twice in an attempt to make them fertile, but without success. White and purple violets, given to me by my sister-in-law, withered at the roots; lilies of the valley and Virginia stock flowered once, then never came again; roses reappeared, smaller and fewer every year. The only growth that did well was anything in nature of a shrub; a purple lilac bush was a perfect heaven of beauty and scent, so were two syringa bushes loaded with starry white flowers that held the dew, while coral red japonica and pale yellow forsythia flourished. If I had the heart to inquire, I might find that the two pink camellia bushes I planted on the back lawn are growing well; but it is better to leave this to conjecture.

No memory of the delightful Baker household is more vivid to me than that of Cad. I used to leave the upper sash of the front kitchen window open at night (with a space too small for human ingress, though adapted to that of cats). When I had no visitor, I used to sleep by turns in the Green Room on the top floor, the larger Lilac Room on the floor below (so called because it was furnished with lilac chintz and had on one of the walls a rather unusual print of Victoria as a Princess, wearing a lilac-coloured dress) or my own bedroom, the first floor front. This had curtains of turquoise blue and a carpet of the same colour; the large bed had an eiderdown covered in rich Tyrean purple silk. In whichever bedroom I was, I would sometimes be wakened after midnight by something jumping on to the bed. I thought it interesting that Cad, having got through the kitchen window and come upstairs in the pitch dark (not that *that* mattered to him), would come to whichever bed I occupied. I was sleeping in my own bed one winter's night when Cad made his way in, his paws covered with liquid mud just above freezing-point. I am ashamed to say that he was allowed to get not only on to, but into, the bed, and work himself downwards to my feet. I reached a hand under the bedclothes and received a very, very gentle nip, which I interpreted as a caress.

This cat's death, at last, was a beautiful case of euthanasia. When he had become so old and weak that he was sleeping nearly all the time, Murray gave him an injection so he died, in comfort and calmness, in surroundings where he had lived since he was a small kitten. His life was another of the enviable advantages that came my way. I fed him when his family were not at home, but otherwise I had all the pleasure of his society without the responsibility for him. As, basically, mine was a one-person household and I was, in any case, away a good deal, I could not keep an animal unless I could take it about with me; a cat would have been impossible, and a dog, much as I would have loved to have one, would have added to my difficulties in travelling, which I always tended to find daunting.

One of my failings is a shrinking from responsibility. I love other people's children, but I have never wanted any of my own. I read some years ago a psychologist's article which said that if women didn't want children, their love affairs were likely to go wrong. The passionate affairs in my life were always with people who could not marry me and came to a natural conclusion. The two people who wanted to marry me appeared to me unillumined and uninteresting. I see now that they were not; it was my unconscious re-editing of their personalities, in an escape measure, which made them seem as if they were. My mother regretted my not marrying; she said to me: 'I should like to see you in somebody's care before I die.' I said, ungraciously, 'You mean you would like to see somebody in *my* care before you die!' My mother said: 'It all comes to the same thing.'

Immediately prior to the outbreak of war, the period of apprehension, expecting air-raids and a general petrification, as it seemed, of normal activities, was much relieved for me by our distant cousin, John Guest. John was homosexual, although at that time this was not openly discussed. He had made a very good beginning in the publishing firm of William Collins, as proof-reader and general assistant, during which stage he had attracted the attention of William Collins himself. A novel which had been accepted was already set up in type; then John noticed that at one point in the action the engine of a motor-car under stress exploded; but in the early stages of the book the car had been given the name of a famous make. This alertness (typical of a very young man who still had the bright intelligence of a schoolboy) saved the firm considerable legal annoyance. Another of his proof-reading feats was not so crucial, as someone was bound to detect the error sooner or later, but if fell to John to point out, in a meeting to consider the 'rough' of the firm's forthcoming catalogue, that it announced publication of the *Gospel of St John*, 'with author's preface'. If this could only have been true!

In those days John took me once or twice to meetings held by a society called Writers Declare Against Fascism; this was what launched me into the shallows of progressive thought. I remember particularly one meeting addressed by Stephen Spender. When it was over, the audience asked questions, to one of which Stephen Spender said: 'I feel very deeply about this, but I am not good at explaining things.' Afterwards a few of us, with myself on the outskirts, collected round him and asked him what war-work he, as a conscientious objector, could honestly undertake? He said: 'I think of going into the teaching profession. I know they need men.' So here was someone who, by his own admission and on his own showing, was not good at explaining things, intending to go into the teaching profession! In fact he was offered the post of English teacher at Blundell's School in Devonshire, in the respectful terms of a contemporary biography 'trying to see whether life as a schoolmaster suited him. It was not surprising to learn that one term persuaded him that he had made a mistake.' Probably his pupils would have agreed. But it must be said that after this he gained a first-rate reputation in a London branch of the National Fire Service.

In the late thirties, I also met C. E. M. Joad, who in the war and the immediate post-war era became one of the best known names in England. This was owing, largely, to the prominent position he took in a weekly BBC feature, a very well-conducted debate on matters of immediate interest called 'The Brains Trust', in which he was by far the most arresting speaker. I knew John Guest would like to meet him and I asked them both to dinner. John said of this meeting, in his obituary on Joad: 'He arrived very late, having spent the day on his farm in the country; he came in knee breeches, with open-necked shirt, carrying a large knapsack. He round cheeks shone, his beady eyes darted about with embracing geniality.' John's own conversation was so interesting and his manner so charming that on learning John was looking for a flat in Hampstead, Joad offered him a second floor of his own roomy, late Victorian house in West Heath Road. The arrangement, a very successful one on both sides, was terminated only by the outbreak of the war. John enlisted immediately; he served in the North African and the Italian campaigns in the 10th City of London Yeomanry and was Mentioned in Despatches. He had said to me: 'Do, do write to me!' I made a point of writing to him once a week. After the war, when I was having dinner in his new flat, in Belgrave Place, he pulled open a drawer and I saw to my astonishment that it was absolutely crammed with letters from me. Then, shutting the drawer, he said: 'Whoever owns the copyright, I have *physical* possession of these letters!'

By that time, Joad's adventures had taken a most unfortunate turn. Coming up to London by rail as he often did, he realised that the London express made a stop for a few minutes at a point on the line below a steep bank that led out of some fields. By posting himself on the bank at a given time, he was able, when the train paused, to scramble down the bank, wrench open a carriage door and seat himself inside. This meant that he made the journey to London without a ticket. This curious practice is hard to account for in a man who made a comfortable income. John was inclined to think that it was related to that part of his character (which made him so stimulating on the Brains Trust) which tended to be always in arms against any people in authority; that, combined with a puckish sense of humour. At the terminus he would wait, inconspicuously, until the crowd at the exit had dispersed, and then wander about as if he were looking for someone, before walking calmly out. Finally an inspector on the train saw him coming in at the carriage door, and exclaimed: 'This train doesn't stop here, sir!' To which Joad responded: 'Then I'm not on it.' This was a neat reply, but it was a mistake: it called public attention to his practice. I think he must have been a marked man for some time. He came before a magistrate and was found guilty of cheating the railway company.

That was only the beginning. Owing to his high news value the case was given wide publicity in the press. Then an official of the BBC sent for him and said that, much to their regret, they were obliged to take him off 'The Brains Trust'; the public demand for his removal was too great. Joad said surely that would die down? It could hardly be serious enough to make his removal necessary. The official took him into the adjoining office, and there were sacks and sacks piled up, full of letters from the public demanding that he should no longer be heard on the air.

The story was so dramatic, so much like something out of folk-lore, that he felt no reluctance in repeating it. I think part of the torrent of public denunciation was caused by resentment among broad sections of the audience who could not resist listening to him but were indignant at his being superior in an unanswerable way. He still had a busy public life, but not long after this he developed cancer of the spine. Some us formed a group to take it in turns to go in and read and listen to him in the evenings: my evening was a Thursday. His companion-housekeeper, known as Maudie, was a remarkable woman, who had had a career teaching in State schools. She was tall and spare and calm and wore always a dress or suit of navy-blue. The first time she let you into the house for the evening, she explained that if the pain came on while you were there, you had to give him an injection. She showed you how to do this, making you practise on her arm. Thank God I was never called on to do it for him. He lay in his bed, in pyjamas and dressing-gown, and though he was obviously ill, his relish for talk was the same as ever. One unexpected change had come over him – his contempt for Christian belief had been well known, but now he was considering it thoughtfully. He wrote to Dr Ellison, the then Bishop of London, who answered readily and came and sat with him during the last weeks of his life. Joad died in 1953.

John came back to London after his demobilisation and returned to a most successful career in publishing. He became literary adviser to Longmans, who had, framed and hanging on their staircase wall, one of the cheques they had written to Lord Macaulay for the History. John's insight and sympathy were invaluable to them in attracting new clients. It has been said that as a result of his activity 'within ten years, Longmans had one of the most distinguished fiction and non-fiction lists in London'. He once said to me: 'Remember, I'll take anything of yours at sight.' I was pleased to hear him say so, but while Victor Gollancz lived, and wanted to keep me, I could not think of leaving his firm.

In 1949 Longmans published John's own war reminiscences, which he called *Broken Images*. It was in the form of a journal, and was based on letters he had written during his service to his close friend, Christopher Hassall, to whom the book was dedicated. The writing is remarkable in many aspects: its simplicity, realistic detail, sensitivity, and the sense of absolute equality with everybody with whom he worked and lived; his description of treatment in a military hospital, the squalor of travelling in packed trains, the exhaustion of working on gun-emplacements, the attacks of enemy aircraft:

Suddenly shouts, everyone scatters like fragments from an explosion. There is a crackling roar, a sound like tearing calico, and there, just above the tree-tops, coming straight at us, the grinning Messerschmitts; rifles, machine guns, all blaze off. Then, suddenly, silence ... the whining note goes higher ... someone shouts: 'They're turning!' The note gets shriller, intenser. A quite ordinary and quiet voice beside me says: 'Down, here they come!' One flattens oneself into a ditch, conscious, for a flash, of the bitter-sweet moment before complete anaesthesia ... the bullets thump into the soft earth and there is a terrific explosion ... Again silence. A rain of falling stones and earth and you say to yourself: 'It's all right, it's all right, it's over.'

In spite of these fearful experiences, wherever he went, in Africa and Italy, he dwelt on the amazing profusion and beauty of the wild flowers. From Beja in January he wrote: 'I wish I could send you a box of these violets beside me, they're singing like nightingales in the candle-light.' From Testour he wrote of 'acres of dazzling yellow flowers, freckled with poppies...sweeping, smooth hills, powdered with flowers, one of them so thickly covered as to be entirely blue'. The passionate observation of the flowers, the vines, the fireflies, is contrasted with the description of the homeward journey, its maddening slowness, its confusion of official orders. 'At last, about four o'clock, the shout from the inner room, "Next please!", meant me.' The most interesting and important part of John's life was about to begin.

Broken Images was published with success in 1949. It won the Heinemann Award. I wished so earnestly that he would do what he had once spoken of doing – write a book about his wild, original, eccentric family, a mixture of North of England tanners, Wesleyan Methodists and an exotic cultivation almost beyond belief and all true. But it was Joad who said to me that good as *Broken Images* was, he did not believe that John would ever write another book. Nor did he.

John died over fifty years later in August 1997, after a life of professional success and as much distress as anyone of his temperament was bound to undergo.

Five

❧

When the elder of my two brothers, Romilly, was six, Mr Kellett at Caldicott gave him his first chess lesson. Later, when my father was seeing him off, Mr Kellett said: 'Your boy will be a scholar.' Romilly fulfilled this prophecy. At Cambridge he gained the Chancellor's Gold Medal in the Classical Tripos.

In 1932 Romilly married Céline Haegler, who was very attractive and intellectually bright. After their marriage she and Romilly spent much time in Athens where he was, first, on the Board of Management of the British School of Archaeology, then a Trustee and finally the Chairman of the Managing Committee. His first published work was *Daedalica*, a description of the fragments of Daedalica sculpture of the seventh century BC. This was very well received, and he was particularly pleased by a notice from the French critic Charles Picard, who congratulated him on the 'précision minutieuse et édifiante de ses analyses'. Monsieur Picard, however, had assumed that Romilly was a woman. Romilly wrote to say how gratified he was by Monsieur Picard's high opinion, at the same time pointing out that he was a man. Monsieur Picard wrote a charming reply, saying he was sure Romilly would regard this error with 'une indulgence souriante'.

I have in my work-box a fragment Romilly gave me: the remains of a horse's head, broken off at the base of the neck, about two and a half inches long. The ears have been rubbed away, a trace remains of the slit indicating the mouth and the large eyes are outlined. The material is like fine powdery pumice-stone, soft and light, the colour a pinkish buff and the surface is dappled with grey, presumably the remains of stain or paint. How I wish I had made Romilly talk to me at length about it. I do remember his telling me that in excavation work you had to be eagle-eyed over the diggers, ready to leap into the trench the instant they uncovered a fragment, their instinct leading them, the moment they had turned up something, to smash it with the blow of a spade.

In 1936 he was appointed Lewis Gibson lecturer in Modern Greek at Cambridge. Romilly was one of the comparatively few classicists who were interested in Modern Greek, and he was therefore approached early in 1938 by the Secret Intelligence Service and asked if he would give up part of the Long Vacations of 1938 and 1939 to learning cryptography. The Government had, by now, recognised that the outbreak of the war was a distinct possibility. The work of the Greek Cypher School would be indispensable to any struggle for Crete, which was, for both Great Britain and Germany, the key air and naval base for the Eastern Mediterranean. The Germans eventually overran Greece and Yugoslavia; only Crete lay between them and Egypt. (My cousin Eve's husband, Kenneth Mackay, was a brigadier in the Royal Engineers. He once told me that before they retired from Crete, he had blown up fifty-three bridges; he felt that for the rest of his life he wanted to do nothing but put on an old coat and talk to gardeners.)

Romilly said that in the first lecture his group had on decoding they were told that in the Babington Plot, Mary Queen of Scots had unnecessarily exposed herself to Walsingham's clerks by using a cipher of her own invention; she would have done better to use one of the elaborate standing versions (though not much better).

In the summer of 1939 my father's cousin Frank Wood took Romilly and me for a motoring holiday in Scandinavia. Romilly had been told by SIS that he was free to go, provided he were back in England by a certain date. He could not tell us anything about this and when our cousin wanted to extend the holiday by another week, he made a determined resistance, for which he could not tell either of us the reason. However, the return was punctually made. Although I had enjoyed the tour, I have only a phantom-like memory of driving through endless forests of evergreen trees, and of transparent lakes coming up to the roadside, lying motionless around enormous boulders. I do, however, have a clear recollection of the museum in Stockholm, which displayed wooden furniture in the classical shapes adopted by England and France in the eighteenth and early nineteenth centuries; but instead of showing surfaces of polished walnut and mahogany, the Scandinavian pieces were painted in pale, ice-like colours: primrose yellow, wild-rose pink, forget-me-not blue. The stops we made at hotels en route to Oslo were of an increasingly agitating sort, because the radios in hotel lounges, kept on all the time, gave out English translations of more and more alarming news.

We got back to London and war was declared on 3 September 1939. Romilly was directed to the Code and Cypher School, Greek Department, at Bletchley. By rather an *ad hoc* arrangement the staff were boarded out in the neighbourhood. At first Romilly was assigned to a delightful farmhouse. When he saw the household cat feeding on tinned salmon and large saucers of cream, he expressed mild surprise as we were already facing the prospect of rationing. The farmer's wife said the cat always had this for his supper, and added: 'You can't explain the war to a dumb animal.'

His next lodging was in a beautiful country house, Chicheley Hall, where the then-famous musical comedy actress Gwen Farrer also had an apartment. She was a friend of the surgeon Sir Ivor Back, and there had been a considerable to-do because when A. J. Cronin brought out his block-busting novel *The Citadel*, in 1937, the villainous surgeon whom he called Mr Ivory was said to bear a strong likeness to Sir Ivor Back. The pre-publication story was interesting. Victor Gollancz said to me about it, much later: 'I read the first half of the script and I didn't like it, but without finishing it, I gave the largest order for a pre-publication print run in the history of the firm.' Considering the caution about libel Victor had shown up till then, this seemed extraordinary, but I believe Miss Farrer gave Romilly the key to it: she told him that when Sir Ivor Back had read the book, he stormed into the office of his solicitor demanding immediate action. The solicitor tried strongly to dissuade him, but Sir Ivor Back exclaimed: 'I'll smash him, if it's the last thing I do!'

To which the solicitor had replied: 'Very well, but it *will* be the last thing you do.' This wise counsel must have prevailed, as no prosecution followed.

The scene in *The Citadel* which describes an operation by Mr Ivory that ends with the patient's death on the table says that just before he began his fatal work, Mr Ivory had never looked so completely the part of the great surgeon of fiction. A portrait of Back by a fashionable portrait painter had appeared entitled *The Surgeon*. His implements are spread out in front of him, and he wears a white coat over morning dress, as used to be the thing; whereas now surgeons appear in linen overalls that leave their hairy arms bare to the elbows. However, as this is all in the interests of anti-sepsis it would be wrong to lament the loss of dignity. The portrait had been exhibited in London and reproduced in the newspapers and Romilly recognised it when he saw it on the wall at Chicheley. It had been entrusted to Gwen Farrer for safe keeping in case of enemy attack on London.

To return to Bletchley: one of the chief consolations to Romilly was that the head of his department was the late Eric Smith; they had exactly the same sense of humour and they afforded each other invaluable support and relief. The work was extremely exacting and the hours thought reasonable for clerks at the beginning of the war had been considerably increased.

Eric Smith had been married to Antonia White, who had a brilliant literary debut with a novel she called *Frost in May*, describing her experiences in a convent school. She followed it with a series of distinguished novels, all of which did well but did not repeat the meteoric success of the first. She insisted on divorcing Eric Smith to make way for somebody else, but neither that one, nor any other, gave her the perfect happiness for which she was looking. She was a most accomplished translator from French, making superb renderings of Colette's novels, and she could have had as much of this sort of work as she chose, but she said it was too poorly paid; she was constantly complaining of poverty. All this information was freely supplied, though from a slightly different angle, by books about her written by her two daughters and herself.

When the Greek Cypher School was removed from Bletchley to Aldford House in Park Lane, Eric Smith was in Antonia's range once more and sometimes found himself taking her out to lunch. These occasions left him in a state of unusual depression, which Romilly deplored – for friendship's sake and because he depended so much on Eric's liveliness and caustic wit for his own enjoyment and support. After their excursions, Eric would return to the office and repeat the lunch-time conversation in tones of deepest gloom. One afternoon this process seemed to be running out of control. 'She kept saying: "I feel I've failed you,"' he repeated, over and over again; she said: "I feel I've failed you."' Romilly could bear it no longer, rejoining 'Well, she has. Let's face it!'

I suppose Aldford House must have been a hotel when SIS took it over. It was a building with a wide entrance hall from which a staircase led up to four successive floors, of which the top floor was the typing pool. The security was so tight that there were guards stationed in the hall and on each of the staircase-landings. The cheerful young typists used to put crumbs of cake and biscuit on the outside ledge of their window for the pigeons, who flocked eagerly to pick them up.

One afternoon a thoughtless girl, finding a heel of cake in the tin too small for a portion at tea, put it outside on the window-ledge. Several large birds converged on it and in their hurry knocked it off the ledge altogether, so that it fell down and down, landing plumb on the black satin hat of an elderly lady who was walking on the pavement below. She looked up, and seeing a group of girls at the topmost window, aghast but laughing, thought that this was a deliberate piece of sauce. Her indignation carried her, resistlessly, through the security guards in the hall, up the first flight of stairs, through the guards on the first landing and she was making her way up the second flight before she was collared and persuaded to come down to the entrance hall again. What pleased the security staff was that she had been gently induced to leave the premises without having the slightest idea of where she had been.

Immediately after the war Romilly, on being released from SIS, was offered the Chair of Modern and Byzantine Greek by King's College of London University. (King's College in the Strand we always called it, to differentiate.) After a long spell of Cambridge life and the enclosed sphere of the Secret Intelligence Service, he enjoyed being in London very much. When he was appointed there was, among other celebrations, a large tea-party to introduce and welcome him.

It was a big room, very full, and I saw, at a distance, the Dean of Canterbury, known as the Red Dean on account of his progressive views. With his pale features and white hair, he gave the impression of a marble statue; it was a pity that he had not the same degree of marmoreal silence. On being introduced to Romilly, he asked: 'Are you married?' 'Yes,' Romilly replied. 'And have you children?' 'Yes', Romilly said, 'I have two boys.' 'How long have you been married?' 'Eleven years.' 'Eleven years?' repeated the Dean. 'You ought to have had more children by now.' I was so horrified when I heard about the exchange with the Dean that I could only ask: 'What did you say?' 'Nothing,' he said. 'I just bowed and walked away.' It so happened that a very sad event had happened in Romilly's home life. Though they had two fine little boys, he and my sister-in-law had always wanted a daughter. During his time at Bletchley one was born, but owing to a run of extraordinary misfortunes, culminating in the fact that heaps of frozen snow prevented the doctor from getting his car out of the garage, she did not survive. It was a dark patch in family life.

In 1960 he and my sister-in-law removed to Washington when Romilly was appointed Professor of Byzantine History and Literature at Dumbarton Oaks. Now officially part of Harvard University, it was then an extraordinarily interesting settlement founded by two married cousins, Mr and Mrs Bliss, each a millionaire, whose hobby was Byzantinism and who travelled over Europe and

Asia acquiring relics of their favourite period, which they placed in a museum in their Georgetown house, Dumbarton Oaks. This became the Dumbarton Oaks Centre for Byzantine Studies.

Romilly was one of those English people who have an instinctive rapport with Americans. He remained at Dumbarton Oaks in the Professorship of Byzantine History and Literature until his untimely death in 1969. My sister-in-law also had the gifts and temperament to understand and enjoy a new scene, a new society. They used to leave Washington in May when the summer heat began, and come back to England, where she went to her family and friends and he spent most of the time based on Downshire Hill.

We seem to have spent so much time in irrepressible conversation at any hour of day or night. I remember coming back from theatres, towards midnight, and sitting talking on the stairs instead of going down to the kitchen to make tea, or, more sensibly, going upstairs to bed. He told me so much, and has left me wishing that I had made him tell me so much more. One thing he imparted (quoted, I think, from Andrew Lang) was the origin of the story of Cinderella. This is said to be of Chinese origin: the reasons for thinking so are the Bride Show (when the Prince wants to marry, all the local girls are summoned to the palace), and the beauty and desirability of exceedingly small feet. The glass slipper was not a Chinese idea; in the original story the slippers were said to be of a kind of fur, the old French term for which was 'vair'. Charles Perrault published his collection of fairy tales in 1697 and when these were translated into English by Robert Samber in 1729, Samber took Perrault's 'vair' for 'verre', and so endowed the story with the enchanting detail of the glass slipper.

Romilly also once pointed out to me that the idea of Paradise conjured up in the Bible is the ideal state of over-driven slaves: nothing to do except to stand about in beautiful clothes, listening to music. That hymn ascribed to Bernard of Morlaix, translated by J. M. Neale into 'Jerusalem the Golden', to my mind threatens a desperately exhausting prospect: 'And there, from care released, The shout of them that triumph, The song of them that feast' – with the brightness of angels, brilliant daylight and the very grass luminous; perpetual racket in perpetual bright light; the idea makes you yearn for dim violets in a silent wood!

As a counterpoise to Bernard of Morlaix, Dr Watts (1674–1748) wrote:

> Then shall I see, and hear, and know
> All I desired or wished below,
> And every power find sweet employ
> In that eternal world of joy!

This idea of expanding our powers seems to me a most inspiring idea of heaven. I wish I had found it in time to show it to Romilly, who would have welcomed it; his chief idea of bliss was using his mind. He would also very much have appreciated, I think, what Dr Watts said in a talk to young men: 'Never let it be said that three little words are too hard for you to say: "I was wrong."'

Over the years when he came on vacation from Washington, Romilly and I had delightful motoring holidays. One was at Winchester, where our principal objective was of course the cathedral. It was transformed into its present visionary loveliness by the bishop, William of Wykeham (1324–1404). Originally the nave was supported on thick Norman pillars, resting on plinths. The bishop did away with the plinths and brought the pillars straight from the roof to ground-level; then he carved each pillar into a cluster of three slender shafts, while the flat ceiling was raised into airy fan vaulting. These effects, down a vista of the longest aisle in England, must be seen to be believed. Another of his works was the founding, in 1378, of Winchester College. When, during the Civil War, a body of Cromwell's troopers burst into the cathedral, they broke open the mortuary chests and bowled the skulls up and down the aisles. They then began to mutilate the effigies on the tombs; but it so happened that two of the officers in the troop, though Cromwellians, were also Old Wykehamists, and they stood, with their swords drawn, before the tomb of their founder. The soldiers, foiled, then turned their attention to the west window;

whatever missiles came to hand they hurled up at the stained glass, until large stretches of it were lying in fragments on the pavement. After the victors had retired, some of the townspeople stole into the cathedral and, on their hands and knees, collected pieces of broken glass. These were afterwards re-set in the window. It was not possible to re-form the pictures the glass had originally held, but the splinters were fitted together and you now see them as a maze of coloured light.

One of the most interesting tombs is that of Cardinal Beaufort, who was also Bishop of Winchester. He was a son of John of Gaunt by Catherine Swyneforde, and he and his brother and sister were called Beaufort after the castle in France where they were born. Catherine Swyneforde had been appointed governess to the children of John of Gaunt's wife, the Duchess of Lancaster, and she took to her duties with such a will that she not only looked after his children by his Duchess, but bore him three herself. I was standing beside the Cardinal's tomb, expounding this story to Romilly while I balanced with one foot on the plinth. Suddenly my foot slipped and gave me an agonising wrench. Romilly said: 'That is the Cardinal saying "I'll thank you to keep a civil tongue in your head when you are talking about my mother."' Laughing as I was, I could scarcely hobble for pain, but we found a chemist nearby who made it much better by applying a lotion and bandaging the sprain tightly. We had to put off further exploring of the cathedral for that day, but the morning after, on going again, I found the slab marking the tomb of Jane Austen, in the north aisle, almost opposite the tomb of the Cardinal. She was buried here on 24 July 1817.

It is remarkable to notice that though the growth of Jane Austen's fame was very slow, steadily increasing until now it is at a flood-tide, it was from the beginning of a high quality. James Edward Austen Leigh, who in 1870 wrote the only memoir of her published by someone who had actually known her, noted with amusement that some visitors having asked where Jane Austen was buried, the sexton directed them, then said to one of the party: 'Was there anything remarkable about that lady? So many people have asked to be shown her tomb.'

In the summer of 1958 we had another wonderful motoring holiday, in Derbyshire. The spring rains had been heavy and the brooks were full; sometimes when we paused on the road, though out of sight of water, we could hear the chime and rattle of pebbles as the streams flowed along. We put up at Bakewell, at a charming hotel, the Rutland Arms; but what was our surprise to see – glazed and framed and hanging on the wall of a first-floor sitting-room – a long statement that Jane Austen had travelled in Derbyshire when working on *Pride and Prejudice*, in 1811; that she had stayed in the hotel and had used Chatsworth as a model for Pemberley. The notice proclaimed:

> In this room, in 1811, Jane Austen revised the mss of her famous book *Pride and Prejudice*. Jane Austen, who travelled in Derbyshire in 1811, chose to introduce the beauty spots of the Peak into her novel. The Rutland Arms was built in 1804, and while staying in this new and comfortable inn, we have reason to believe that Jane Austen visited Chatsworth, only three miles away, and was so impressed by its beauty and grandeur, she made it the background for Pemberley, the house of the proud and handsome Mr Darcy...any visitor to Chatsworth must be struck by Miss Austen's faithful portrayal of the scene.

The notice goes on to say that Jane Austen's description of hills, wood and water are unmistakably drawn from personal observation of Chatsworth and its immediate neighbourhood: 'so when visiting the hotel and staying in this room, remember that it is the scene of two of the most romantic passages in *Pride and Prejudice*.'

Every word of this is fallacious. Jane Austen's life is unusually well documented by her letters to her sister Cassandra and by copious family tradition. There is no mention of her 'travelling in Derbyshire'. Her nearest recorded approach to the district was

[86]

when in 1806 she visited the rectory of her cousin Edward Cooper, at Hamstal Ridware. She and her mother had come on from staying at Stoneleigh Abbey in Warwickshire, and Hamstal Ridware was described as being 'just over the border' into Staffordshire. This cannot be called 'travelling in Derbyshire'. Dr Chapman, to whom I telegraphed, reply paid, in my agitation, confirmed that there was no evidence of her ever being north of the Trent.

I wrote to the Stretton Derby Brewing Company who owned the Rutland Arms, and had a most courteous reply, saying that the notice was the work of Mrs Davie, of Stanton Park, Matlock. Someone from the company wrote to Mrs Davie, asking if she would so kind as to give the Jane Austen Society her grounds for these statements. She replied that she had read that Jane Austen had travelled in Derbyshire in 1811 in the Official Guide to Bakewell, published in 1936, the author of which was now dead, but she insisted that Jane Austen's description of the hills, woods and river at Pemberley was exactly that of Chatsworth. In fact these features are as they appear in various prints and Jane Austen had, from childhood, been familiar with Gilpin's work on picturesque land-scapes. Gilpin published, in his series of *Picturesque Tours,* that on the Lakes in 1789. Mavis Batey, in her admirable *Jane Austen and the English Landscape,* says: 'Pemberley is a fictious literary land-scape, created in the same way that Gilpin said he composed his picturesque landscape; ideas are taken from the general face of the country, and not from any particular scene.'

Mrs Davie might have stated that her identification of the Pemberley landscape with that of Chatsworth was the result of personal visiting of the latter, but how anyone who had both read *Pride and Prejudice* and visited Chatsworth could think the latter an impression of Pemberley only shows to what lengths enthusiasm for one's ideas can carry one. Jane Austen describes Pemberley as a 'large handsome stone building standing on rising ground'. It had a picture gallery and a saloon. 'The rooms were lofty and large, and the furniture suitable for the fortune of the proprietor.' It was clearly the large country house of a man whose fortune was said to be ten thousand a year. But ten thousand a year, even in the 1800s, would not have gone far to maintain Chatsworth: Chatsworth is a palace. The Revd R. Ward, who published an early-nineteenth-century guide to Derbyshire, gives some idea of its size:

> The building is in the form of a square containing a court, within it having a fountain of Orion seated on a dolphin in its centre and a colonnade to the north and south sides...the south front is 190 feet long and is enriched with plasters...the west front is 172 feet long, and enriched in a similar manner... over the colonnade to the north side of the quadrangle is a gallery nearly a hundred feet in length, the walls are covered by an assemblage of drawings by the most eminent masters.

The size of the building surely makes it impossible to suppose that the resemblance of Pemberley to Chatsworth is so strong; it could only be a distorted inference accounted for by Jane Austen's personal presence in Derbyshire?

When Romilly had gone back to Dumbarton Oaks he found in one of the Sunday papers an illustrated feature, by Mr Denzil Batchelor, on the Rutland Arms which, based on Mrs Davie's notice, had outdone even her: 'There on the first floor, is [Jane Austen's] room, her book-case is still on the wall, her desk by the window where, in 1811, she worked on *Pride and Prejudice*.'

I told Romilly that I thought of writing an article on the whole matter for a forthcoming Annual Report of the Jane Austen Society. He wrote in reply:

> 'Yes, it was abominable, but it was so interesting to me because it was a splendid illustration of the growth of a legend, such as we find so frequently in lives of saints, for example. In fifty years time, this stuff will be appearing as fact in official biographies of Jane Austen, and in a hundred years time it will need a real effort of scholarship to eradicate it. Do put it down if you can.

I put the matter to the Committee of the Jane Austen Society and they agreed that we ought to publish a refutation of Mrs Davie, so I did my best, with the heading: 'Growth of a Legend'.

As I have said, Downshire Hill had two rooms on each floor, although on the top floor my father had divided the front room into a bathroom and a small front sitting room. The latter was, as a rule, my writing room; it was particularly agreeable, with a grate that drew uncommonly well and an outlook through the Gothic sash-window into the treetops. When the moon was bright I would fly up to the top storey and turn off the light to get the benefit of the moonlight through the gothic panes, throwing shadows of the glazing bars across the floor.

When Romilly was at Downshire Hill, the writing room was his and became known as the Scriptorium. He also had the small back bedroom on the top floor known as the Green Room. He could have had the more commodious Lilac Room on the floor below but he preferred the Green Room as, besides being next to the Scriptorium, it gave you, as he said, a stranglehold on the bathroom.

The Scriptorium had a small Victorian writing desk under the window; also a small armchair with a padded and buttoned back, now covered in old-rose plush. It was of the kind called a boudoir chair, and had belonged to my father's mother. Romilly was very fond of it. When I came in at the door, he was often sprawling in it and his contented glance would meet me, over the top of the book he was reading. I was very much struck by an evidence of his scholarly habits that I had never had the opportunity to notice before. There had come to me, from one of our aunts, a collection of letters written to our grandparents on the death from smallpox of their son Romilly Ingram, a missionary who died in India in 1898. His radiant cheerfulness and his devotion to his cause had made a lasting impression on the people who knew him. I made him the chief figure in my novel *Brightness* and I had so many letters from readers that one could sense how striking he must himself have been when this shadow of him had so much appeal. The collection included my Uncle Romilly's letters to his parents. In a moment of unusual seriousness he told his mother that parting from his home was so painful that he 'could not have made the sacrifice for anyone but God'. The illness was brief and the death very sudden; all the members of the family, as well as family friends, wrote to my grandparents, and all the letters had been kept. I had arranged them as well as I could, thinking, indeed, that I had done it well. Romilly had said he must look through them and one morning I left them with him while I went out to the shops. I shall never forget the impression I received when I came in and saw them on the Scriptorium table as he had arranged them: the envelopes in such close-pressed packs, the packs laid out so neatly, 'it was a world to see'. It was the more impressive because he had little sympathy with that branch of the family and had performed the work merely as a scholar.

His most important works were, I believe, translations and commentaries of which the most valued was *Byzantium: The Imperial Centuries AD 60 -1071*, which he published in 1966. Dr Robin Cormack, of London University, said of it: 'The best recent history of its kind; a masterpiece of lightly-worn scholarship, by a great stylist.' This was a highly specialised book for students of the period, but in 1961 he produced a work that aroused considerable public interest. This was *The Dilessi Murders,* an account of the kidnapping and murder in Greece in 1870 of four prominent English visitors. It resuscitated a *cause célèbre* which at the time had caused much excitement and indignation but had afterwards lapsed into oblivion till Romilly brought it to light again. He devoted one chapter to Greek attitudes towards truth and objectivity which generated almost as much heat in Athens as the original affair had done in London; but which was regarded within the British Embassy as so perceptive that one ambassador there told Romilly's son Michael (at one time also a diplomat) that he made a point of always giving it to read to new arrivals at the Embassy.

He inscribed this book to me with a dedication saying that without my encouragement it would have not been written, and without my advice it would have been much worse that it was. I cannot believe that I gave advice, which I was not competent to give, and which in any case he scarcely needed, but I believe that what I did was to *listen,* and it is strange how few people there seem to be who are prepared to do this. Victor Gollancz was, but he was in a class by himself. Others begin by being all attention; then something you say reminds them of an experience of their own, and they veer off, breaking your thread, until it is better not to attempt to renew it. I am so glad that, without being aware that I was so, I was useful to Romilly, when I thought I was simply being engrossed.

At what turned out to have been the last of these halcyon visits before Romilly's untimely death of heart failure in 1969, he said he would like to take back to America with him one of my finds in the purlieus of Camden Town and Chalk Farm: a portrait a little less than life-size, of the head and shoulders of a gentleman in mid-eigh-teenth century manner. He wore a scarlet coat with the light blue sash of the Garter across it, and the Garter Star very high up on his shoulder. I had thought it might be a portrait of Prince Charles Edward, the Young Pretender, Bonnie Prince Charlie, who claimed the English throne as a grandson of the excluded James II and was utterly defeated at Culloden in 1746. I took the picture to the National Portrait Gallery and sent in a request to see someone who could identify a portrait which I thought might be of Bonnie Prince Charlie. I was visited by an impressive official who took the picture from my hand and said, 'Oh yes, that's Bonnie Prince Charlie.' He pointed out that the Garter Star's being so high up on the shoulder was the result of an effort to get the insignia into the portrait; the size of the canvas would not allow of the Star's being placed in the proper position, over the heart. He thought this supported the idea that the picture had been painted (no doubt among numerous others) to distribute to the Young Pretender's followers. (As Romilly said, there was, of course, no possibility of Charles Edward's having been awarded the Garter, which is in the gift of the Sovereign.) For a while, in his scarlet coat, he made an interesting addition to my red and white dining room; but when Romilly said he would like to take the picture back to Dumbarton Oaks with him, I was more than pleased that he should.*

Romilly died very suddenly. I never saw his will, but I think the picture must have been covered by a clause leaving his prints and pictures to Harvard. If so, I am glad to think of its being there, by his request.

* I find the relics of Bonnie Prince Charlie are of more interest than I had thought. *The Daily Telegraph* of 3 July 1999 reports that a six-inch fragment of tartan worn by him was sold for £2,000, three times its expected price, at a sale in Edinburgh. Romilly judged better than I did.

Six

It had been odd to find, in 1932, that there was no biography of
Caroline Lamb; it was perfectly astonishing to find, in 1935,
that there was no complete life, including chronological discussion of works, of Jane Austen. The present tide of biographies,
with films and television productions of the novels, will make the
statement almost incredible to those whose interest in Jane
Austen's stories developed only in the present age of popularisa-
tion; but then, though Jane Austen's reputation was as high as it
is now, the number of her admirers was infinitely smaller. The
main sources of information about her were, first and foremost,
the edition which I earlier mentioned by Dr R. W. Chapman, published by the Oxford University Press: the six novels in 1923, the
two volumes of letters in 1932, and *Jane Austen: Facts and
Problems*, and *Jane Austen: A Critical Biography*. Dr Chapman's
work represented the highest standard of scholarship and critical
insight.

There were, of course, the brief biographical notice written by
Henry Austen in his preface to the posthumous edition of
Northanger Abbey and *Persuasion;* the fascinating, but all too
brief, memoir by her favourite nephew, James Edward Austen
Leigh, and the outlines of a biography, with a selection of her
letters, by the descendants William Edward and Richard Arthur
Austen Leigh, *Life and Letters of Jane Austen*, published in 1913.
But this also, though of great interest so far as is goes, does not say
much about the novels or relate them to the background. Otherwise the material on Jane Austen was of a fragmentary kind
(*Aspects of Jane Austen, Jane Austen: Her Homes and Friends*),
though all most useful for the details they provide; but one longed
to find a book that told one everything one wanted to know (so far

as any book could be expected to do this). In the end, I wrote the book I had been looking for.

The earliest reviews were not encouraging and some were both tepid and denigratory; not that the reviewers thought that they knew more of the matter than I did, but because they felt it was a dead bore to have to read about Jane Austen at all. It was reviewed with cold kindness by Dr Chapman who was, then, only an awe-inspiring name to me; but, over the years, an increasing number of people have told me that it gave them what they wanted. The memory of two comments has always given me particular pleasure: Lord David Cecil called it 'invaluable' and in a series called 'Books That Have Changed My Life' Anna Massey wrote that she had read it on the seashore, feeling it had done just that.

The publication had for me one momentous consequence. In 1940 I had a letter from Dorothy Darnwell who lived with her sisters on top of the long hill leading down to Alton. This was the little country town about a mile from Chawton, the village where Jane Austen had spent the last eight years of her life, in the small house where she had revised *Sense and Sensibility* and *Pride and Prejudice*, and composed *Mansfield Park*, *Emma* and *Persuasion*. Dorothy's letter said that this house, Chawton Cottage, was the property of Captain Knight, the direct descendant of Jane Austen's brother Edward, who had taken the surname Knight when his adoptive parents made over to him the estates of Godmersham in Kent and Chawton Great House in Hampshire.

The cottage stands at the junction of the Gosport and Winchester roads; there used to be a large pond at the crossroads (since drained). When in 1816 Jane Austen wrote to her nephew Edward mentioning the anxiety he had had over his mother's illness, she said that presently a little change might be good for him, and she hoped his physicians would order him 'to the sea-side, or to a house beside a very considerable pond'. Cassandra Austen died in 1848, and on her death a sale followed in which most of the contents of the cottage were dispersed, chiefly to members of the family and their descendants. Dorothy said that if it were known that there was a place to display them, people who owned these relics might either sell or give them to us; at all events, we would stand a chance of finding out what these objects were and who possessed them. When she was assured, as she often was, that no idea of the kind could be attempted till the war was over, she always maintained that the scheme must be made known as widely as possible; in time, interest in Jane Austen would do the rest.

Dorothy's work in the founding of the Jane Austen Society was such as only she could have done. She knew the district thoroughly and, as a countrywoman, she could make herself welcome in the neighbourhood. The interior of the cottage was then divided into three tenements, let at half a crown a week. Miss Stevens, the oldest tenant, was eighty in 1940. Her mother remembered skating on the pond by moonlight. Old Mrs Stevens also remembered the gardener from Chawton Great House; he was then an old man who wore a smock and a tall hat; he had helped Jane Austen to transplant a sapling oak from the park to the garden hedge that overlooked the Winchester road. Miss Stevens identified the tree for us: 'the third on the Winchester road'. We put a board on it, saying that it had 'traditionally' been planted by Jane Austen; but some few years later the local boundaries were redefined, and the hedge was declared to be under the auspices of the Hampshire County Council. They cut the tree down.

What Dorothy wished was to form the Society whose object should be, ultimately, to buy the cottage from Captain Knight and to make it available to such members of the public as wanted to see it. What set the scheme at work in her mind was the sight of the cast-iron grate which had been wrenched out of the Austen's dining room to make way for the tenant's gas fire, and was then lying on the scrap heap of what had been the village forge. Dorothy alerted Mr W. H. Curtis, the Keeper of the Alton Museum (that wonderful collection of the relics of country life before the supremacy of the Industrial Revolution). She asked him if he would shelter the grate in the museum until we could restore it to its original site. Mr Curtis agreed with pleasure. When we formed the Society, he was our first chairman.

I was glad that Dorothy lived to see this grate restored to its proper place. The room on the right of the front door is identified as the dining room by a letter from Mrs Knight, saying she had heard from a gentleman travelling in a post-chaise past the house who had seen the Chawton party 'looking very comfortable at breakfast'. Originally there had been a sash window on each side of the front door, but when his mother and sisters moved into the cottage, Edward Knight blocked up the left-hand window opening into the large room, which made the family living room too public, and opened another, looking into the garden.

We held our first committee meeting in the living room of the Darnwells' house in May 1940. Of Dorothy's two sisters, Elsie was an invalid, but Beatrix was vigorous and capable to a degree. She had been the Secretary of the Royal College of Music. The Alton branch of Lloyds Bank acted as our treasurer, but Dorothy said: 'I must have Beatrix with us in some capacity. I can't do without her.' So Beatrix became assistant treasurer; Dorothy and I acted as joint secretaries. We began our financial arrangements on a yearly subscription of half a crown. The money was used in postage and printing of an Annual Report, very meagre and on flimsy paper. Mr Curtis presently advised our raising this to five shillings, which we did, but this caused Dorothy a pang because she felt that the village dressmaker would not now be able to afford the membership. Dorothy's earnest, tactful and altogether welcome approaches on behalf of the Society meant that by 1946 we had gained the interest of just the people we needed. The Duke of Wellington, whose country seat, Stratfield Saye, made him an influential figure in Hampshire, consented, on Dorothy's representation, to be our President. I then wrote a letter to Dr Chapman, telling him of our aims, and of how far we had got by then, and of what benefit it would be to the scheme if he would give it his approval. Much to our satisfaction he replied that he was very glad to hear about the formation of the Society, and added: 'Thank you for making so much of me.'

In December 1946 *The Times* published an article describing the Society and its aim. This caught the eye of Mr Edward Carpenter, a retired solicitor; he and his wife (a niece of Kate Greenaway, for whom she had often posed for some of the latter's child pictures) had been thinking of founding a charity in memory of their son, John Philip Carpenter, lieutenant in the 1st Battalion, East Surrey Regiment, who was killed leading an attack at Trasimene, aged twenty-two.

Mr Carpenter now decided that he would buy Jane Austen's house and create the Jane Austen Memorial Trust in his son's memory. He bought the house from Captain Knight for £3,000 (we ourselves had collected £1,100, but Mr Carpenter told us to spend this on repairs to the roof and windows). He persuaded the village library to vacate the Austens' living room and presently found acceptable alternative accommodation for the tenants, without which the law would not have allowed him to end their tenancies. On 22 July 1949 the house was formally opened by the Duke of Wellington; he and Dr Chapman had made speeches to an audience of 400 in a marquee pitched on the lawn of Chawton Great House; after which several hundred of us walked or went in cars down the road to the house, and the Duke unlocked the living room door. This was an exhilarating moment for the Committee.

From then onwards, Mr Carpenter made Jane Austen's House, next to his family, the most important object in his life. He not only maintained the fabric, but he kept in review all announcements of sales and auctions, and bought objects either with a reliable pedigree from Jane Austen or of particular period interest, such as the neat little box of ivory squares, each engraved with a letter of the alphabet, of the kind used in the 'Letters' game by Frank Churchill, Jane Fairfax and Emma. (In fact the Hartfield set must have been made of pasteboard instead of ivory, since Emma herself inscribed the letters on the squares, old Mr Woodhouse 'fondly pointing out how beautifully Emma had written them'.)

[97]

Mr Carpenter engaged a succession of admirable caretakers who lived in the house and managed the business of admissions, which increased steadily, as Dorothy had always said it would. It is very satisfying that his second son, Tom Carpenter, himself became resident caretaker.

It was decided in due course that the Society's Committee should leave all financial matters to the Trust (which we were more than glad to do), and that the Society should be responsible only for the production of the Annual Report and for the arrangements of the Annual General Meeting. The Society, besides printing the address of the guest speakers at the AGM, has also published, over the years, a series of articles without which no present biography of Jane Austen would be complete. The most important of these was the one we were allowed by the *British Medical Journal* to reprint: Sir Zachary Cope's article, 'Jane Austen's Last Illness', which, from details in her own letters, he diagnosed as Addison's Disease, a tuberculous affection of the liver capsules. Addison did not give a name to the illness till 1855, when he published his *Essay on the Disease of the Supra Renal Capsules*. Sir Zachary Cope collated all Jane Austen's references to backache, faintness, vomiting, discolouration of the face, with characteristic intermittent spells of feeling better. He said that many diseases might cause one or more of these symptoms, but only Addison's Disease would account for their all being present together. This terminal illness had been speculated upon by all previous writers on the subject, but no one else had discovered the complete answer to the enigma.

Information less valuable, indeed, but very interesting of its kind, came to me through Hoare's Bank. Ronald Griffin told me that the accounts of the Revd George Austen and his wife as well as those of Cassandra and Jane and Mrs Leigh Perrot were all with the bank and he would have the ledgers laid out for me to look at. One of the unremarkable books about Jane Austen had said that the account of her having been at the Abbey School at Reading rested on unconfirmed tradition only. The first page of

Mr Austen's account that met my eye recorded his payment for the half-year for his two daughters to Madam de la Tournelle, the Abbey School's headmistress. Another interesting item was the payment by Mrs Leigh Perrot to her sister-in law Mrs George Austen of £50 a year. The Austen family had been dismayed by Mr Leigh Perrot's will, which left everything to his wife, with the proviso that his nephews and nieces should receive £1,000 at her death. Of the two sons who had contributed to their mother's support, Edward was threatened with an expensive lawsuit and Henry was bankrupt; Francis and Charles had families of their own and little to spare. Some unfavourable criticism has been made of Mrs Leigh Perrot; she was rich already and the Austens were almost poor; but her account shows that from the date of her husband's death, she made these annual payments. We published this also.

While we were still so primitive that we had possession only of the living room, we were anxious to replace the ugly modern fireplace with something simple but of the period. We then had our first experience of what we had been warned to expect: that once a society, however modest, is known to be solvent, other people will try to clamber onto the raft. An acquaintance of one of us said that an artist who was a friend of his had a chimneypiece of Adam design which would be exactly suitable, and we could have it for £40 (a considerable sum for those days). Dorothy arranged for it to be sent to the house and I saw it, propped up against the living room wall. The first thing we all noticed was that it was covered with flowers, sprays and flourishes; it was very 'late' Adam and not a thing that would have been found in a small house, comfortable but simply furnished. But there was no need to talk about taste: it was obvious that the piers were too long, raising the shelf at least eighteen inches above where it ought to be. When Dorothy told the go-between, regrettably, that it was too ornate for our purposes, he replied that it was Adam, as if that disposed of the matter; and when she further explained that it was at least eighteen inches too tall, he said we could cut eighteen inches off the base. We were being asked for £40, in money of the time, on the ground that the chimneypiece was Adam's own design, and then being told to cut eighteen inches off the base!

As time went on, the house became more and more like a home of the period 1810–17. The first treasure we acquired was a plain, elegant bureau-bookcase which had come from Revd George Austen's rectory at Steventon, probably one of the earliest pieces of furniture with which Jane Austen had become acquainted. I used my influence, for what it was worth, towards keeping out everything of a date later than Jane Austen's death. There are small, inspiringly arranged museums, one knows, all over the country, but one feels the one established at Chawton must be among the most evocative and charming.

The audiences at the Annual General Meeting continued to grow in number and now packed the marquee. The proprietors of it had already told us that, after several enlargements, it could be enlarged no further. When we heard this, I could not but remember our first meeting in the Darnwells' living room, all five of us. We had the benefit of Sir Hugh Smiley, first as secretary, when he smartened up the proceedings of our enthusiastic but somewhat ragged AGM with military precision; he then undertook the chairmanship. The success with which he discharged the office could be gauged from the groans that broke out all over the audience when, after thirty years, he said he must retire.

For the AGM of 1975, the bicentenary of Jane Austen's birth, we had an exhibition arranged in the large upstairs room of the house, traditionally known as Mrs Austen's bedroom. A doctor attending Henry Austen, an acquaintance of the Prince Regent's librarian, the Revd Stainier Clarke, told the latter that the author of *Pride and Prejudice* was now in London, nursing her brother. The Prince Regent instructed Mr Stainier Clarke to get in touch with her and invite her to see the library at Carlton House. In his letter Mr Stainier Clarke said: 'The Regent has read and admired all your publications.' He added that if she liked to do His Royal Highness that honour, she was at liberty to dedicate her next publication to him. Jane Austen had, in private letters, expressed strong disapproval of the Regent's character, as concerned his treatment of his wife: 'poor woman, I shall support her as long as I can, because she *is* a woman and because I hate her husband. I am resolved at least always to think that she would have been respectable, if the Prince had behaved only tolerably to her at first.' But the favour was too valuable to refuse.

The forthcoming publication was *Emma*. John Murray had the three volumes specially bound for the Prince Regent and sent to Carlton House, carefully timed to reach their destination before publication. The volumes, now in the library of Windsor Castle, were lent by the Queen to the Society for the exhibition; the spines of the three volumes, like all the books in the Prince Regent's library, had had, deeply cut in them in gilt, the Prince of Wales's three feathers.

Besides this treasure we had also on view the topaz crosses bought by Captain Charles Austen out of prize-money as presents to his sisters; these and some unpublished family manuscripts (including an address by James Austen to the family cat 'who had eaten a piece of steak reserved for the author's luncheon') were arranged in a glass-topped case. As the jewels and the volumes of *Emma* were uniquely valuable, Sir Hugh had arranged for two retired police inspectors to be on duty in the room during the hours when the exhibition was open. The case was locked and they took charge of the key. The exhibition was crowded with visitors and only one slight contretemps occurred. A lady with most respectable credentials, writing a work on Jane Austen, wanted to examine the manuscripts at close quarters. She made her wishes known in a forcible manner, stating her claims to preferential treatment, and her right to have the glass case unlocked for her just for the very brief time for which she asked; she did not want to study the manuscript, just to verify a few points. She almost commanded the inspectors to open the glass lid. The crowd surged round, agog at this struggle. Whatever the justice of her claims, the one fact made clear to everybody present was that when two police officers undertake to keep something locked, it stays locked.

The friend who warned us we would be in danger from people who wanted to climb on board would have found a grim satisfaction at the one which threatened us in 1993.

An energetic member of the Committee, to which he had asked to belong, propounded a scheme by which the Society should buy the house, 4 Sydney Place, in Bath, where after leaving Steventon the Austen family had lived from 1801 to 1804. It was to serve as a museum, a shop for the sale of 'Austen Books' and a 'Centre for Jane Austen Studies'. It is not clear what this term implies: if it means biography or social history, then the library required by the student would have to be on the scale of those provided in public libraries. These, unless they are the result of collections presented to the library (as the library of George III was presented to the Reading Room of the British Museum), are founded by a long process of accumulation; they are not conjured up at will.

The promoter of the scheme outlined the expenses to be incurred: £250,000 for the freehold of 4 Sydney Place and £275,000 for its restoration and conversion. We were told that 'once planning permission had been obtained, the Society would launch a national and international appeal for £900,000, supported by media publicity of every kind'. The statement went on: 'The effort must be dedicated and unremitting and our aim might take several years to accomplish. We recommend that the Committee should undertake this project as one within its aims and capacity and which will stimulate the Society's energy, reputation and growth.'

As far as I and other members of the Committee were concerned, there was little need for a new project to 'stimulate the Society's energy, reputation and growth'. Our sole object had been to gain possession of the house, acquire for it by degrees such objects as had an unquestionable pedigree as being connected with Jane Austen, and open it to the public. That we had done. Maintaining it to the best advantage was all we wanted to do. It was a relief to hear from the trustees of the Jane Austen Memorial Trust that they would not agree to Mr Edward Carpenter's money being used for any project except the one for which he intended it. I speak as the only surviving Founding Member of the Jane Austen Society.

Seven

＆

Victor Gollancz was a source of intellectual and physical
replenishing. He would take you to lunch, usually at the Ivy
or the River Room at the Savoy, to hear from you how you were
getting on with the book on which you were at work. Victor was
a most generous host, but when the menu cards, the size of pillow-
cases, were put before one, he had first to decided on his own
lunch; it had to be delicious, naturally, but also, equally important, it had to be adapted to his constitution. I remember Victor
intently studying the *carte* at the Savoy, his eye running over the
whole acreage in dead silence, a sort of mystic concentration,
while the head waiter hovered at his elbow and the junior one
stood by, eyeing me with affectionate pity. When this matter was
finally adjusted, one was cordially invited to choose whatever one
fancied. The problem was too extensive for me; when the head
waiter had made a suggestion, I closed with it thankfully; then this
stimulating occasion was in full swing. I always found that when
I was telling him something, it became clearer in my own mind,
standing in a stronger light and with some significance hitherto
unrealised, which developed in the telling. To myself, I called this
feat on his part 'creative listening'. I have experienced it with a
few other people since, but he was the first one to make me
conscious of it.

Besides these lunches, which were of high voltage, there were
brief business interviews, up what looked like attic stairs in the
Henrietta Street premises of Victor Gollancz Ltd, where everything was so severely practical and sparse it gave you a feeling of
exhilarating professional stimulus. Then, in dizzying contrast,
were the parties Victor gave annually at Claridge's. A splendid
buffet at the end of one of the two or three rooms into which the

party overflowed was piled with luxurious dishes; in a small room an orchestra was discoursing, in the *salon* the talk was incessant Babel, which had a sort of eager desperation about it. On one occasion, between two or three in the morning, the orchestra in the small room where there had been dancing, began to play the National Anthem. A number of us were crowded round the walls of this smaller room. Naomi Mitcheson, a well-known author of the times who wrote novels in a period of ancient Greek history, was apt to appear, when *en fête*, in the costume of a Greek peasant, in bulging bodice and bunchy skirts, with plaits of hair over her ears and stalks of corn sticking out of them (a taxing costume for most figures, but people have to decide these matters for themselves). At the first, unmistakable bars of the Anthem, Naomi Mitcheson scuttled across the polished floor so that everyone should remark her gesture, and as the rest of us were singing the Anthem, she sat down, plump. I told one of our friends this, who, not long afterwards, found himself in a theatre audience in which Naomi occupied one of the stalls. When the orchestra began the National Anthem, he nearly threw himself over the rail of the dress circle, hanging over to see if she were going to make this demonstration of intellectual honesty again, but to his keen disappointment, having got up from her seat, she came quietly up the central gangway in the most bourgeois manner imaginable.

At one of Victor's heroic literary parties I also met Rose Macaulay who was a combination of scholarly distinction and sharp observation and wit. She was very tall, slight and elegant, and so gracious and friendly it filled one with awestruck delight. I met her fairly often after that. One memory of her is particularly vivid to me. We went to a theatre together. As most people have at some time or other, I had had a rather long spell of hospital visiting; it was November with dark, rainy evenings and my back use to ache as I climbed into the bus. However, I used to say to myself: 'Never mind, St James said you had to!' This was because, with characteristic inaccuracy, I thought I remembered that St

James, when running over the actions that were inseparable from true religion, had included visiting the sick. When I looked at the passage again, I found that he had never mentioned it. In the theatre interval, as we sat in the brilliantly lighted auditorium, full of people talking gaily and exchanging views, I said: 'St James must be having a good laugh at me!' and told her why. She laughed too, then she said: 'But after all, Someone Else did say you had to, didn't He?' I can't describe what my sensations were at that moment; it was a kind of supernatural consciousness, which made me want to shiver.

Another of my recollections of Rose concerns Vera Brittain. She had been at Somerville with Vera, whom she had found, and continued to find, exceptionally trying. Vera Brittain, after a long and wearying initial failure, had had a resounding success with her autobiography, *Testament of Youth*. Launched, she went on to a flourishing career, though none of the subsequent books equalled the *réclame* of the first one, in which the subject, her experiences as an army nurse in the 1914 war were so deeply felt and so important in themselves, they overpowered any personal elements. The subject floated her. She became a star on Victor's list; but she was now inclined to compensate herself for past struggles and disappointments by being somewhat captious and overbearing. This, as you will suppose, did not go down well with Victor, and, before the publication of one of her books, he delegated a pre-publication interview which he would ordinarily have conducted himself to his then partner, Norman Collins. At a small party, Norman described this interview; he related that Vera Brittain had said: 'When you have my sort of chocolate-box prettiness, it's very difficult to get men to take you seriously.' Norman said to us: 'I kept looking at her, and wondering what on earth she meant.' This was a good story and of course it got a laugh; but then Rose said, rather sternly, 'That's all very well, Norman, but when she was at Somerville she was *very* pretty, very pretty indeed.'

When my novel *The Tortoise and the Hare* was published in

1954, Rose was on a BBC Committee which discussed recent fiction. This was, in terms of financial success, my best novel, but I encountered some severe, personal criticism from readers who felt that the interest of the book was too much confined to one class, not to say to one income bracket. I was told by a young man, a student in a university society to which I had been asked to give a talk, that what was wrong with the book was that it wasn't about anything that really mattered. As I felt that the suffering caused by the break-up of a marriage was something that did matter, I asked him, in surprise, what were some of the things that really mattered? After a pause, he said: 'Well, trade unions.' Some of the speakers on the air held a view similar to the young man's, though more fluently and pungently expressed. One of them said, in withering tones: 'All this, about gracious living!' The centre of the book was a brilliant hard-natured man, the woman's husband, and her ten-year-old son who was completely remote from her, and I felt this criticism was altogether unfair. I was listening to the programme and was so glad to hear Rose exclaim: 'Gracious living! What do you mean by gracious living? Evelyn wasn't very gracious, Gavin wasn't gracious – do you just mean that they had enough to eat?'

In the period immediately after the war, while living with considerable parsimony, I was very glad to have an offer from Victor Gollancz Ltd to read scripts for them, at a rate of two or three a week. I was on the middle rung of readers: the lowest was formed of secretarial staff, who could see at once if a script were useless; I and others formed the next rung, and on our level it was only occasionally that we sent up a script saying we submitted it for very serious consideration, which meant that it would be read by Victor himself or a trusted associate. Sometimes we said we did not think a script was up to publication standard, but that on pages so-and-so there were pieces of such good writing the firm might like to tell the author they would be interested to see his or her next work. Of the very few one could recommend for consideration at the top rung, the only one I can remember in any detail was the original form of John Braine's *Room at the Top*. When I saw it, it was called 'Joe for King' and written in the third person. The change to the first person was, I assume, owing to the tremendous success of Kingsley Amis's *Lucky Jim,* related by the hero Jim Dixon. Fortunately for me I recommended the book; if I had not done so, in the light of future events, I daresay my employment as a script-reader to Messrs Victor Gollancz Ltd would have been abruptly terminated. Victor was a genial man and fond of me, but his dictum was that he didn't pay people to make mistakes. However, in submitting the script I said that I thought it needed some alterations, of which the one I remember best was that Joe's parents were excellently drawn at the beginning of the book but were never mentioned again. I thought the reader would expect a final glimpse of them.

After the script had been refused by eight publishers the book appeared as *Room at the Top* and was a runaway success. I got hold of a copy, and remembered enough of the original to recognise the alterations it had undergone. I noted that my suggestion of a final sight of the parents had been adopted, also that the love-interest had been greatly strengthened, I suppose somebody else's advice. When the first wave of success was at its height, I read that at a public dinner given for John Braine he had proposed a toast to the eight publishers who had turned the book down. I felt that he might also have toasted the publishers' readers, who must have played some part, however trifling, in his success.

Very few of the scripts would be recommended even for a partial consideration. The chief impression I retain from all this reading is how very well people who have no real capacity for writing can, when venturing into autobiography, nonetheless describe their own childhood. Over and over again one would say to oneself: 'Surely *this* one is a winner?' Only to find that when the writer reached his or her adult years of education, love-making, professional experience, the whole thing weltered down into a waste of dullness that no one would read unless they were absolutely obliged to.

But a public is there, ready to be interested in the discipline and routine of callings or professions outside their own. Bacon said: 'I hold every man a debtor to his profession', and this calls up a vivid reminder of that wonderful development of mental skills, acting and reacting between the practiser and the practice. Bacon gives the reader innumerable flashes of perception: the one about allowing the witness to tell the story in his own way comes, not as you might expect in the essay on judicature, but in the one entitled *Despatch*, where he says that if you try to keep the teller strictly on the point, 'he that is put out of his own order will go forward and backward and be more tedious while he waits upon his memory than he would have been if he had gone on in his own course'.

Bacon was called a 'natural philosopher' because of his interest in science, but the most fascinating aspect of his writing is his piercing observation of human nature. From another angle it is keenly interesting to read that Sargent, uniquely famous in his era as a taker of likenesses, used to say to his students: 'Look three times at the subject for every once at your canvas.'

The term 'reportage novel' covers not novels which introduce a professional background to the main story, but those of which the first-hand description of a profession or trade is the vital essence of the work. In the late 1930s there were number of early examples of this form: *I'm Not Complaining* by a state school teacher, *Coming, Sir* by a waiter, *It's Cold in Front* by a taxi-driver, *Can I Help You, Madame* by a vendeuse. The writers were obviously practical people who were probably swept into Government employment at the beginning of the war. As far as I know, none of them wrote anything afterwards.

Nonetheless three reportage novels were published, almost within a year or two of each other, which, at the very top of achievement in this form, set the model for other works in the same genre: *One Pair of Feet*, about hospital nursing, by Monica Dickens, *Doctor in the House* by Richard Gordon, and *The Painswick Line* by Henry Cecil, a highly comic view of the legal process and the Law Courts (the *fons et origo* of John Mortimer's television series, 'Rumpole of the Bailey'). These three writers, besides their acute sensitiveness to telling detail, and their humour seen against a background of understated seriousness as regarding nursing, doctoring and the law, have, each of them, a high degree of competence in characterisation and brisk movement. Among the qualifications necessary in this type of work, though, you must be minutely familiar with the routine you describe but not so immersed in it that you have lost all sense of detachment.

Once, while I was in the Ministry of Information, I had to go down on some errand to the basement where printed matter was stored. The afternoon tea reached us, on my floor, between quarter to four and quarter past. The tea-lady brought it round on a trolley, with the urn and a fleet of cups, and no real timing was possible because she had to bring up the trolley in a lift and wait till one of these was vacant. I had got down to the cellarage and made my business known to some of its inhabitants, when one of them, a nice elderly man with grey hair, wearing a neat khaki-coloured overall, beautifully laundered and ironed, total strangers though we were, got us into a passionate argument about the authorship of Shakespeare's plays, leading off with some quotation to which he added: 'As the man from Stratford is supposed to have said.' We were whirling madly in full spate when the lift doors opened and the tea-trolley emerged: at half past two in the afternoon. 'Goodness!' I exclaimed, breaking off: 'Does your tea come round as early as this?' A rather bored-looking woman said, in matter-of-fact tones, 'It comes about now', from which it will be deduced that she could never have written a reportage novel, she had become dulled to the strangeness of her lot.

On ceasing Government work, I made up my mind that I would return to giving my time and nervous energy to writing. I decided to write a reportage novel myself. The school at which I got the best part of my education, St Christopher's, Letchworth, and the one at which I had taught, the King Alfred School in London, were in ethos so similar I combined recollections of them both. I called it *Young Enthusiasts*, a quotation from Dr Johnson's *Vanity of*

Human Wishes – 'The young enthusiast quits his case'. The head-mistress of King Alfred School, Violet Hyett, was one of the most remarkable beings I had ever met; you did not feel you were work-ing under her authority (which, however, was absolute) but more as if you were a young painter working in the studio of a master. Then, again, I had been immensely lucky in the headmistress of St Christopher's, Isabel Boag King. In *Young Enthusiasts*, knowing she had been dead many years, I reproduced her as the head of the school I described. I represented her as a widow, calling her Mrs Cortwright, feeling that this would do away with any recognition, but all the touches of educational genius and sympathy I conveyed were copied from or inspired by Miss King. The book was a success, but to my surprise at an Annual General Meeting of the Jane Austen Society, two young women I'd never met came up and said how much they'd enjoyed *Young Enthusiasts*; then one of them added: 'And all that about Aunt Bell.' It was very agreeable, but also startling.

I was thinking so intently about the development of the reportage novel that when the English department of Aberystwyth University invited me to give a lecture I chose this subject. The animated discussion which followed confirmed me in thinking that it was one of general interest. In preparing the talk, I had been led to think about 'process', and found how absorbing Benvenuto Cellini's memoirs are, with their minute descriptions of his work as a goldsmith and jeweller. When he was meaning to make a particu-larly fine type of inlay he wore his right arm in a sling the whole of the previous day, in case any casual knock should injure the perfec-tion of its balance. (This reminds one of the manual dexterity of the surgeon Astley Cooper (1768–1841) who, operating in an era with-out anaesthetics, when the longest time a patient could survive under operation was fifteen minutes, was famous for 'an eagle's eye, a lady's hand, a lion heart and the speed of a greyhound'.) One of Cellini's most interesting passages describes how he made a clasp for a cloak for Pope Paul III, setting an exceptionally large and bril-liant diamond. His Holiness invited designs from Cellini and a rival goldsmith, his only stipulation being that the design must be in the form of a circle. Cellini describes his rival's design: in the centre of a circle, God the Father is sitting, with the diamond in his breast. You are just thinking how impressive this must have been, when Cellini wipes out your admiration by describing his own design. The circular form is defined by flights of angels; in the upper half, God the Father is sitting, with the diamond under his feet. What a lift of spirit that gives you!

I have spoken of the reportage novel as, in my view, the most interesting development in fiction of the twentieth century, but one ought to remember that the first example of the form was in fact published in 1719. It was a minute description of how you keep yourself alive if you are cast up, alone, with a few ship's stores, on a desert island.

The reportage novel inevitably raises questions of legal liability for libel, as indeed do all works of fiction which are other than pure fantasy. I have often recalled the incident of the late Rosalind Wade's first novel, *Children Be Happy*, which was published by Victor Gollancz in 1935, very early in his publishing career. It was the most successful book she ever wrote, though she had a moderately profitable career afterwards with other publishers. Once, over lunch, Victor gave me an account of his side of the affair. He had realised that, as a first novel, the book must necessarily contain a good deal of personal experience, but he had supposed that she must have employed the usual screening devices: that when she said the school was in the Cromwell Road, of course he thought it wasn't, but it was; and when she said there were two headmistresses, one of whom had an artificial leg, he took it for granted that there weren't and that she hadn't; but there were, and she had. In the end he had to pay damages to the two headmistresses, the school matron, two members of the staff and one of the girls, a débutante whose presentation occurred at the same time the book was published. Although he was insured against libel, he still had to pay £2,000, which was a large sum in those days. The book was withdrawn so hurriedly I would never have seen it, but my brother David, who was then with a firm of London solicitors, saw in the Law Report of *The Times* that the action was pending and went out and bought a copy.

The result of this episode, so far as the rest of us were concerned, was that when Victor Gollancz accepted your script for publication you had an interview with his solicitor, Mr Harold Rubinstein, who was very kind but of course extremely searching. He only once, in the eddies of the crisis caused by Rosalind Wade, asked me: 'This Mr So-and-So: do you know anyone at all like him?' I said: 'I did once, but it was a very long time ago.' Mr Rubinstein said, pensively: 'A very long time ago? I'd rather hear that he was dead.' But in the end he allowed the matter to be passed over.

The question is almost coeval with the development of the novel as a highly popular form of entertainment, and when *Bleak House* appeared in 1854, with the character of Mr Harold Skimpole immediately calling Leigh Hunt to mind, poor Leigh Hunt's cry of 'But I thought he liked me!' touches on something which lawyers will brush aside, but novelists recognise as an extremely subtle issue – the relationship between the living person and the fictional re-creation evolved by the novelist who, having laid the groundwork of a perfectly recognisable character, has been led on to develop it on lines that are offensive to the original. This mixture of reality and imagination is responsible for some of the most brilliant effects in great novels, but the writers have usually maintained that no one could be more surprised than they that any reader should think their fictitious character copied from life. This state of immixture can become positively ridiculous. One well-known author was reported in *The Daily Telegraph* of July 1996 as speaking resentfully of people who criticised him because he had described living persons in unmistakable detail, moving in a circle equally identifiable, and describing himself and them as taking parts (usually disagreeable) which they never acted in real life. His reply to the protests of his victims, and on general princi-ples, is: 'I assumed that if I could take liberties with myself, I could take them with other people.' He goes on: 'The whole premise is that you take real people and put them through their paces.' He ought to have had a stiff dose of Mr Harold Rubinstein, and so he would have, if the original firm of Messrs Victor Gollancz had been his publishers.

Eight

In 1946, after *Young Enthusiasts* had come out, I had an offer from Mr Wadsworth, the literary editor of what was then called the *Manchester Guardian*, to review books for him. I did this for about two years. The one over which I worked hardest was Dr Chapman's *Jane Austen: Facts and Problems*, being the printed version of his Clarke Lectures which he had given in Cambridge. I was of course severely limited as to space, and I worked to the uttermost of my capacity to celebrate the exceptional qualities of the work within these limits. I was rewarded by a postcard view of Oxford, on which was written: 'Thank you, RWC.'

I also recall the number of novels that came my way by Angela Thirkell. It was a very interesting professional experience to have to read carefully works so widely popular, by a cultivated writer, which one found abhorrent. My reading of them coincided with my horror of Marxism; I recoiled from them in indignation because they seemed so amply to justify the abuse and contempt poured on the middle classes by Marxist writers. I re-read one of two of these novels lately, and my impressions of them were even stronger than I remembered. I still admired, but with a more developed professional insight, the light touch and airy pace, and the easy capacity to place characters before the reader, but I was again chilled by the writer's insensitivity, amounting almost to moral idiocy. One of her characters complained that now there were no members of the family still in the armed forces the posts were so dull: it used to be so nice to get letters from the Front; a remark only to be equalled by one from a character in another work, who, complaining of the wretched quality of the cakes, said that one might as well be still in the war again. Mrs Thirkell's very interesting group of immediate ancestors included Rudyard

Kipling but this heredity, in her written works at least, was not evident.

I had letters from so many people, agreeing with, or taking up points in my reviews, that I was not prepared for a brief note from the office of Mr Wadsworth's successor, saying that they would not be sending me any more books to review. I thought it odd that they did not even say thank you, but perhaps they were too busy to spend time on courteous nothings. I had felt stimulated by the work, but it had been a strain, and now that it was removed, I was able to concentrate on a commission I had from Sampson Low, a firm known to me only by name, to write a collection of biographical sketches to be called *Six Criminal Women*. The title was rather louche but I was allowed to make the selection. I began with Lady Ivie, to whom M. R. James had given a walk-on part in 'A Neighbour's Landmark' in his *Ghost Stories of an Antiquary*. This was a real person, who made an impudent attempt to appropriate land left by will to somebody else and was tried by Judge Jeffreys. I then chose Jane Webb, the famous pickpocket who called herself Jenny Diver, and was introduced under this name in *The Beggar's Opera*; and thirdly Florence Bravo of the Balham mystery, which I afterwards expanded into a full-length novel, *Dr Gully*.

The best of the remaining three was Madame Sarah Rachel Leverson, who in 1863 opened a beauty parlour at 47a New Bond Street, which she entitled in gilt letters 'Beautiful for Ever', at a time when make-up was considered beyond the pale for respectable women. But she made a fortune selling good paint, and by relying on the unwillingness of respectable women to undergo the publicity of bringing her into court for fraud. When she was at last tried for fraud and blackmail, she received a prison sentence, but on her release she began the business again, and again made a fortune. Finally, she was sentenced to gaol once more, in the course of which sentence she died; but her assistant had given evidence in court that the salves and precious essences were compounded of carbonate of lead, starch, fuller's earth and hydrochloric acid, mixed with water from the pump in the backyard. I was able, through a dealer in antique books, to get a copy of Madame's brochure, bound in glossy rose-pink boards with the title *Beautiful for Ever*. This contained not only her spin-off, on the sacred duty of women to make the most of their beauty, but gave a list of the preparations Madame could supply. These included: pure extract of China rose, Alabaster Liquid, Arabian Perfume Wash, Balmy Reed Tooth Powder, and Jordan Water from the pump. I have lost so many precious books to borrowers over the years that I have long since taken a vow not to lend any (or hardly any). My first severe loss was inflicted by a young man who wanted to borrow the brochure *Beautiful for Ever* to help him with an article he was proposing to write. When, after an ominously long time, I tried to recover it, the girl who had introduced him to me said he had left the address she had known and she had lost sight of him.

I next wrote what turned out to be the best-selling of all my novels, *The Tortoise and the Hare*, epitomising two types of women: the hare, a married woman, attractive but unpractical; the tortoise, the neighbour with few outward attractions but with strength of purpose. Victor Gollancz said: 'If you will do precisely what I tell you, I will make it our big book for 1954.' Of course I agreed, and the process was not too painful; it consisted simply of cutting out passages. He said I was too apt to lead the reader up to a crisis and then start away on some other track. I followed his directions exactly, but even then I submitted my final version of the manuscript to him with considerable trepidation, writing to him that 'it seems to me now quite empty of the amount of feeling I thought was in it, and if you think it unsatisfactory and not likely to do... it would be far better to cut one's loss than have something really bad attached to one's name.'

I had numerous letters from women, most of whom had seen themselves as hares, though a few defended themselves being tortoises. I also had a strange experience some years after the publication. I was in Foyle's second-hand department, and found myself in front of a copy of the book, which I drew off the shelf, opened at random and began to read. For about ten minutes, I should think, I entirely lost the sense of where I was, and read on and on, as if the book had been written by somebody else. I had wholeheartedly agreed with Victor's wishes about the cuts, but I don't think I had quite realised, until then, how much the book owed to him. I have never looked at it since; it marked an era to which I had no desire to return.

Inspired by the example of Sampson Low, Odhams Press then asked me to write a sort of companion-volume to *Six Criminal Women* which they decided to call *Ten Fascinating Women*. I thought the title was abominable, but I could not move them, as I was not able to suggest anything else. However, I much enjoyed working on this collection: it included Harriet Wilson, Elizabeth Inchbald and Sarah Jennings, Duchess of Marlborough, which last was, I think, one of my better pieces of biographical writing; but I did not think that either publisher knew his business very well. I asked Victor Gollancz despairingly if he would take over the two collections and make one volume out of the best sketches in both. He was kind, but he said he did not like to handle short stories or books of essays. He urged me to set to work at once on some full-length book for him, and added: 'If you need money, tell me and I'll see you get some.' I never knew how he would have done this as I never asked him, but I felt reassured by his promise. Another publisher, with whom I was having a non-committal lunch, told me he had liked some of the sketches very much but, he said, 'That form is the most extravagant way of using nervous energy you could have hit on; you have to use as much force as you would on a full-length biography, and you have to do it six, or ten, times in succession.' I will not do it again, but I do not regret having lavished my energy on *Ten Fascinating Women*, both because I had so much enjoyed the work and because the publication of the second book led to the most interesting and exciting publication of my life.

I had chosen, among the Fascinating Women, Elizabeth Tudor from childhood to her accession. Curtis Brown, my agents, offered the book to the American publishers Coward-McCann. They did not want it, but they said that if I would make the sketch of Elizabeth into a full-length biography, they would be glad to commission that. I told Victor, who approved of the idea immediately and said he would commission it too. He attached considerable importance to simultaneous publication in England and America, and in the course of discussion, I don't remember why, he said: 'We may have to hold them up a little in America.' I could not but be secretly amused, seeing that he had rejected the book which was the origin of the undertaking, but naturally I was delighted that he now took a proprietary interest in the scheme.

Elated, I settled to work in the Reading Room. Though I had long been much interested in Queen Elizabeth, I have never felt anything like the excitement produced by reading the documents of the reign, chiefly in the *Calendars of State Papers* – domestic, French (calendared under 'Foreign'), Spanish, Venetian. The value of the *Calendars* is not only the details they supply, of conversations, rumours, appearances, but the fact that they are written by ambassadors who are trying to relate the actual truth, so far as they can perceive it, to their own Governments. The *Calendars* were all in a row on the open shelves, together with another mine of priceless information, John Nichols's *Progresses of Queen Elizabeth*. These give not only accounts of the Queen's entertainment at the universities, by civic bodies and at the houses of nobility, but also lists of the presents that were given to her on New Year's Day, of jewellery, ornaments and precious objects. They also include the Wardrobe Lists for every two years. These settle the question of how many dresses were found in the Wardrobe at the Queen's death: quoted, variously, by other (more modern) authorities at one to two thousand. The items, added up, give a total of nine hundred odd, but many of these are what we should call separates: bodices, skirts, cloaks, each of which is counted as 'one'.

A topic not only of absorbing personal interest but of first-rate historical importance was that of the Queen's refusal to marry, which hardened into the cult of her virginity. In the early years of the reign, Lord Leicester told the French ambassador, de la Forêt, 'I think, if she married an Englishman, she would marry me. But', he added, 'I have known her better than any man alive, since she was eight years old, and from that very time, she has always said: "I will never marry."' Elizabeth's kind and charming stepmother, Catherine Howard, was executed in 1542 for adultery. In that year Elizabeth was eight. The episode of the Queen's beheading was made more frightful to those who heard about it by the fact that when she was arrested at Hampton Court the King was at Mass, and in an attempt to reach him, she rushed towards the chapel, shrieking wildly, till the guards pulled her back. She was beheaded as her cousin Ann Boleyn had been, and buried in the Tower chapel of St Peter ad Vincula, near her cousin's grave. Leicester's words to de la Forêt have often been quoted, but I think I was the first person to point out that this execution was performed when Elizabeth was eight. The execution of her mother when she was two no doubt had a powerful effect on her subconscious mind; the effect of the second one was on the fully conscious mind of an exceptionally intelligent child of eight. 'I will never marry,' she said. It was her comment on her mother's fate and the fate of her mother's cousin, both of whom had married her father and were now lying, headless, in their graves.

The result of this murder of the normal sexual impulse was the exaggeration of minor aspects of it: an abnormal passion for men's admiration, and a close relationship in which it was understood that the man's passion was never to be gratified. Like the other qualities ascribed to Elizabeth, this one had a providential influence on her success as a sovereign. The complicated foreign policy of England demanded perpetual defence against Spain and France: Spain, from Philip's determination to subdue the independent Dutch provinces, so that he might make the Netherlands a base from which to control the whole of Europe; France, until the execution of the Queen of Scots in 1587, as the possible launcher of an invasion of Scotland on her behalf, from where the French army would pour into England, spiriting up any disaffected Catholics as they came. A most useful tool in the English negotiations with France was the long-drawn-out pretence on Elizabeth's part of willingness to consider a marriage proposal from the younger of the French princes, the Duc d'Alençon. During the period of Elizabeth's reign, from 1558 when she was twenty-five till the early eighties when she was obviously incapable of child-bearing, the Government's pressing anxiety was to see her married and the mother of an heir, as their only preservation, in case of her death, from invasion or civil war. Sir Thomas Smith, Secretary of State who was also Ambassador to Paris, whose letters give most likely notes of conversations with the Queen, wrote a Dialogue between two contestants: one of whom he called Wed-Spite, the other Philoxenes (the Philosopher). Wed-Spite urged the dire peril to the state which would arise if Elizabeth were to marry, and die in child-bed; and his opponent, Philoxenes, reminded him of all the women who survive this ordeal 'so merrily, so quietly, in their fine beds of down' and look so beautiful after it, to say nothing 'of what haste they make to go to battle again'.

I have never seen this passage quoted by anyone else writing of the reign, and I would never have found it but that, roaming in front of the open shelves, I came across a brief biography of Sir Thomas Smith, included in the collected works of John Strype on Tudor documents.

An uncouth person once said to me, after reading my book *Elizabeth the Great,* that 'she was a great one for indoor games'. That cannot be denied; but one would like to say, in this context, that two leading historians who were Catholics, Bishop Lingard and Lord Acton (the premier English historian of his era), were quite without the vicious spitefulness that distinguishes many of the lesser Catholic historical writers. Lingard said he had examined the evidence for Elizabeth's reputation for wild and promiscuous lewdness, and he did not find the charges made out; but, he said, if you make a habit of receiving men in your bedroom when you are in negligée, you have only yourself to thank for what people say about you. As he puts it: 'The woman who neglects the safe-guards of chastity must be content to forfeit the reputation of chastity.' No one can say fairer than that.

In 1990 the Folio Society brought out *Elizabeth: A Life from Contemporary Documents* by Maria Perry, which for the first time gave the answer to the problem which had perplexed everybody up till then: she published the source of Elizabeth's speech to the troops, drawn up at Tilbury in expectation of the landing of the Spaniards from the Armada. This is one of the most brilliantly successful speeches the Queen ever made, but everyone had wondered how it came to be preserved, as it was delivered orally, with an appearance of the impromptu, and how it could be audible to anyone not in the foremost ranks. Maria Perry found that Leicester did have a copy of the speech, which he gave to one of the military chaplains, Dr Lionel Sharp, telling him to re-deliver it to the ranks who had been too far off to hear it in the Queen's voice. This solved the puzzle, I believe, for the first time in 440 years.

My book was published in 1958, 400 years after Queen Elizabeth's accession. Its success was due to Queen Elizabeth rather than to me. My father died a few months after its appearance. I was so glad he lived to see that, recalling that early introduction to Creighton's *Queen Elizabeth,* I had dedicated it to him.

Nine

My mother took me to Stratford when I was sixteen. Till then I had, unthinkingly, accepted the idea of Shakespeare's stature; it was not until I first saw some of the plays at Stratford that I began to realise it for myself. Since then, every time I open one of the greatest plays I am almost knocked down, sent flying by piercing recognition.

I had once seen Ellen Terry when I was about ten, and my mother took me to a matinée of *Romeo and Juliet*, in which Ellen Terry played the Nurse. I remember the surge of applause which greeted her first appearance; one of the highlights of the performance was her fierce indignation with Mercutio, exclaiming 'Scurvy knave!' After his exit she breaks off what she is saying to Romeo to interject 'Scurvy knave!' She does this twice in the text, but Ellen Terry did it three times, if not more, taking a step or two in the direction in which Mercutio had disappeared, rapping angrily with her stick. The audience were laughing their heads off. The other high point was when she came to wake Juliet on the bridal morning, exclaiming: 'Why, lamb! Why, lady! Fie, you slugabed! Why, bride!' The last word was such a peal of encouragement and congratulation and love, it made the discovery even more piteous. I wish I could remember her rating of old Capulet. What I do recall is her superb delivery of how Juliet, as a child of three, had fallen on her face and raised a bump on her forehead, 'and it cried bitterly'. Shakespeare knew that when a child has hurt itself, it will stop crying if you can distract its attention. The nurse's husband picked Juliet up and said: 'Fall'st thou upon thy face? Thou wilt fall backward when thou hast more wit; wilt thou not Jule?' And, by my holidam, the pretty wretch left crying, and said "Ay."

During my first, enchanted, visit to Stratford, the company was led by Baliol Holloway and Dorothy Green. They were both highly successful at Stratford, where Ba was, for years, the centre of an enthusiastic cult. They never quite gained star status on the West End stage, though throughout the Twenties Ba was idolised at the Old Vic; his tall, broad-shouldered but gaunt figure, his inimitable voice which reminded you of the echo of waves sweeping into a cavern, were not suited to the sophisticated light social comedy of the era. He was, however, very successful in the Shakespeare seasons in the Regent's Park Open Air Theatre (which he described as 'half-salary and double pneumonia'). Someone who brought a Russian friend to the Regent's Park production of *As You Like It*, in which he played Jacques, said that the Russian had declared that he had never seen, and had never expected to see, on the English stage, anything like such an impression of philosophy and melancholy.

Most actors, I suppose, are very good raconteurs. Ba was. He was extremely fond of Gilbert and Sullivan's opera, and he told me that once, as a schoolboy, he had made his mother give him the money for a seat at a Savoy matinee – I think it was *The Yeoman of the Guard*. He said Sullivan himself was conducting with a white flower in his buttonhole. Before the overture his score slipped off the stand and several members of the orchestra stooped to grab it. Ba also told a story which I do not think is in print. Gilbert was telling Sullivan his idea for the story of *Iolanthe*. He said: 'The young man is half a fairy.' Sullivan said: 'Which half?' Gilbert, furious at being interrupted, exclaimed: 'What does it matter, which half?' Sullivan said: 'I should think it matters to Iolanthe.'

In the years immediately before the war, Ba had a very good season under the management of Sydney Carrol, who leased the Ambassadors' Theatre, small and very conveniently sited just off Leicester Square. Here Ba produced *The Rivals*, in which he played Sir Anthony Absolute and Lady Tree played Mrs Malaprop. After this he produced Wycherley's *The Country Wife*, in which he played Mr Horner. This obscene and delightful comedy had a most successful run. He produced and acted in these eighteenth-century comedies with a sense of period that was positively illuminated by his physical presence. As Charles Lamb said of William Smith's performance of Charles Susface: 'he took the eye with a certain gaiety of appearance.'

But none of this was enough of what he wanted. The gnawing misery of an actor who has a following and a well-founded confidence in his own powers, but sees the steadily ebbing tide, 'by chance or nature's changing course untrimmed', the long pangs of disappointment, the suffering of what is felt as a continual, undeserved rejection, are dreadful to experience, even at second hand. Ba had always said he wanted a play about King Charles II. Arthur Bryant had succeeded with one about Pepys, *And So to Bed*, in which Charles had an important part but not the lead, and there was room for another. I undertook, under Ba's supervision, to write one. The chief interest in the one we projected was the episode between the King and his favourite bastard, whom he had created Duke of Monmouth, and who betrayed him – seduced by Lord Shaftesbury into a plot to assassinate the King, after which Monmouth himself would reign as Shaftesbury's puppet. The discovery resulted in the hurried banishment of Monmouth to save him from execution for high treason.

It was extremely interesting to me to work with someone so steeped in theatrical experience. Sometimes, when I thought a scene had reached its climax, Ba would produce a further one. Very interesting, too, was that when he felt the dialogue should be a little longer at a certain point in the scene, he hadn't the words but he would beat time for as long as the few extra lines would last. He got the play put on at the Theatre Royal at Windsor for a week, with himself in the lead. I was thrilled by every minute of it. It had such packed houses that when Lyn Harris, the headmaster of St Christopher's at Letchworth, where I had had most of my education, tried to get a seat on the last night (which I am sure I could have got for him if I had known he wanted to come) he was told they were sold out.

Anyone who has had a play considered for the West End will know all of this story – the highly distinguished names who almost accepted it, the times success was almost in the bag and then evaporated. One near miss was an approach from Ivor Novello. He was still at the height of his theatrical success, but told me that the time was coming on when he wouldn't be able to sing and dance any more, and he wanted a full-scale romantic part in which he could graduate into a serious phase. He had seen the play at Windsor and he said that if I'd given the chief part to Monmouth instead of to Charles II, he would have bought it as it stood. He asked me if I could rewrite it, to arrange that? I said yes, and rewrote the script, enlarging Monmouth's part by the inclusion of Lady Henrietta Wentworth, with whom Monmouth had a passionate love-affair. Ba of course helped me with all this, and we hoped that Novello would cast him as Charles II. The final disappointment was acute, but even then I could see how interesting it was from the professional point of view. Ivor Novello said, after reading it: 'I can't do it, I'm too old, I could come on and hold it up for ten minutes, and after that, no one would believe a word I said.'

There was, however a treat in store: under the title *King Monmouth*, which was what the wretched young man allowed the mob to call him, the BBC made a gripping radio version of it. Ba was an acclaimed Charles II, supported by an excellent cast, and the music from Purcell's *Dido and Aeneas* emphasised the emotion. Ba and I were listening to it in the little glass box in the studio. Norman Wright was then one of the BBC Directors of Drama. This was the first time I had met him, but later I had the delight of a friendship with him and the actor Robert Harris. When Norman heard that I was in the listener's box, he came to speak to me; he said it had made him weep: 'I cried over it.' The production was so successful they repeated it twice.

In Ba's last years, after the death of his devoted wife who had had, it must be admitted, a good deal to put up with but never failed in her admiration and love, his loneliness was acute and he used to do a great deal of walking, on Hampstead Heath and in

Regent's Park. He always had a dog; the most appealing was Joey, a golden labrador, with all the graciousness and affection of its kind. When Ba had taken a walk over Hampstead Heath, he would come to my house for coffee, or chocolate, and as soon as I opened the front door, Joey would walk in. One morning Ba had been walking in Regent's Park when Joey, with amazing suddenness, shot away and disappeared. As he never left Ba's side in the normal way, this was not only distressing, but mystifying. Ba sought him all over that area of the Park, and at last came up with a park keeper, whom he asked how he should set about finding his dog. The keeper said: 'He'll come back to you; dogs often bolt just about here. When the wind's in a certain quarter, they go mad with fright: they can smell the lions in the zoo.' He was right; Joey returned and he and his master continued their walk.

Penelope Turing came into Ba's life in its last phase – a long-time admirer who had just been introduced. As a journalist she had reported the opera at Bayreuth and other events of musical importance, and she published an unusually attractive autobiography and two collections of essays. She was part of one of the later *cultes* of Ba at Stratford. We met each other in his flat. Ba said to me afterwards how gratifying it was, at his time of life, to have met this elegant, charming creature as a new friend. The doctor found a male nurse for him, who was off duty from teatime till 9 p.m., and Penelope and I took it in turns, during the last few months, to sit with him during these hours, and give him his tea and supper. (We got for him an excellent Jaeger dressing-gown from the Actors' Benevolent Fund.) On one of the last evenings he said to me, his beautiful eyes looking at me so kindly: 'What is your name, my darling?'

During the last two years of Ba's life I would meet Donald Sinden at Ba's flat. Don was then approaching the height of his success, and his affection was a major solace to Ba in his wilderness. On the first occasion of our meeting I had come on one of my regular visits and found Don sitting with him. Don quite soon took himself off, and I stayed well over an hour. When I went downstairs to the front door, I found Don outside, sitting in his car. He had waited all that time to ask about the details of Ba's care and see what could be done. It was he, at the last, who made the arrangements for Ba's memorial service, in St Paul's, Covent Garden (known as the Actors' Church). Donald Wolfit chose the words to be inscribed on the memorial tablet:

> Your name is great
> In mouths of wisest censure (Othello, II, iii)

Ba had a long-standing estrangement from Edith Evans, dating from before the time I knew him and made more bitter on his side as her success increased while his declined. I never heard the details from him, but from what I could make out, the trouble began from her first season at the Old Vic, which coincided with the era of his greatest success there. In her youth she had been of large frame and when playing Kate Hardcastle she had apparently thought to reconcile this appearance with the part by interpreting it, not as the pert serving-maid the text suggests, but as a bouncing country girl. Ba had tried to modify this conception by reminding her of the words of the text which describe Miss Hardcastle in her disguise as a 'pretty, spritely little thing', but apparently Edith Evans had found the suggestion impossible to adopt. I have read some typed copies of the press notice of the original production of *She Stoops to Conquer*. None of them was enthusiastic about her; they implied that with the support of an actor of Baliol Holloway's gifts and experience, she would presently develop a highly promising performance. This in itself started the association off on the wrong foot. I never heard any circumstantial account, but Ba, on the only occasion when he spoke to me of the matter, intimated that there was no possibility of any reconciliation; he muttered some explanation to the effect that 'something had hit her where she lived', but as she chose to relinquish the connection he would not attempt to re-establish it. From the time I knew him they were never in touch, but she came to his memorial service. As I had never met her, I did not feel able to speak to her, but the sight of her, in one of the front pews, all in black, looking pale and distraught, was strangely comforting.

In the years immediately after the war I was fully occupied looking after visitors, writing my contribution to the new literary form, the reportage novel, and the brief life of Henry Fielding which I contributed to Dame Una Pope-Hennessy's series of *The English Novelists*; but I hungered for some work on the BBC. I had had a little experience in broadcasting, but only in brief features; I wanted more. Orwell had once written scornfully that if all you wanted was an income, broadcasting or television would serve your turn.

But would they? How did one get oneself on to their field of vision? I did not know how to start the process. In this state of mind, I was one day rung up by a young man – young by the sound of his voice, which had, however, not only a foreign accent but an intonation of indescribable *hauteur*. Someone at the BBC had given him, or suggested to him, a commission for a feature on English dramatists of the Victorian era. This person had given him my name as a source of information, and he was now telephoning me to find out who the Victorian dramatists were. I was more than surprised, but I ran off one or two names: Henry Arthur Jones, I said, Wilde, Pinero. The voice said, and its superior tone was now tinged with scorn: 'And who is PINAIRHO?' Heaven help us, I thought, why didn't they give the commission to *me*, instead of to this party, who has to ask *me* who Pinero was? I said, as collectedly as I could: 'He was a very successful and well-known late Victorian playwright. His most famous play was called *The Second Mrs Tanqueray*, but you can find out about him and his works in your local branch of the county library.' Then I rang off. I used, in those days, to read the *Radio Times* regularly, and I kept looking through it for an announcement of this feature on late Victorian dramatists, but it never appeared. I suppose his well-wishers had been able to boost him as far as getting him the commission, but beyond that, their resources had failed him.

The advantage to me, however, of this singular conversation was that it inspired me to look up references to *The Second Mrs Tanqueray*. I found that Graham Robertson (the brother of the then famous Shakespearean actor, Forbes Robertson) in his memoir, *Time Was*, recounts that Sir George Alexander, the actor-manager of the St James's Theatre, who had already accepted Pinero's play, was at a loss to find, disengaged, any actress suited to the part. He asked his wife and Graham Robertson to make the round of the London theatres to see if they could discover an actress who could present the heroine of this – essentially dated – but intensely moving play. After many wasted evenings, they found her at the Adelphi, a young, inexperienced actress who was already under notice from the management as being dangerously incompetent; but the experienced eyes of Graham Robertson and Lady Alexander recognised that they had found the Second Mrs Tanqueray: her name was Mrs Patrick Campbell.

Though her powers were not in dispute, her awkward temperament as well as her inexperience made rehearsals a nervous business. On the first night Pinero was too much agitated to sit through the performance; he left his box and went out to walk in the soothing darkness of St James's Park. When he returned to the theatre, he found that the curtain was being raised and lowered and raised again in response to the demands of an audience whose enthusiasm had created pandemonium. Mrs Patrick Campbell did not realise that she was the chief cause; no one stopped her because no one realised what she meant to do – which was to go quietly back to her lodging where her two children were asleep in the care of the landlady.

The emergence of this great actress on the night of 27 May 1893 was as sudden as the bursting of a rocket into arabesques of brilliant fire. 'For twenty years', James Agate said in her obituary, 'she had the ball at her feet', but her unfortunate temperament, which made a startling appearance in the course of her success, caused her to take keen delight in vicious teasing or actual cruelty to other people and made managements, in the end, decide that she was unemployable. It brought about her professional eclipse. Agate said: 'She kicked the ball away and it rolled out of reach.' Mrs Tanqueray exclaims at the height of her anguish: 'The future is only the past, entered by another gate.' These dreadful words remind one of a theory of those two psychoanalysts who were extremely fashionable in the 1950s, Ouspensky and Gurdjieff. They said that certain people act like gramophone needles on a faulty record: they go on and on repeating their mortally damaging mistakes, except when, in rare cases, some terrible shock jerks them out of the groove.

I made this material into an article for the then successful magazine, *Women and Beauty*. They gave it the title 'The First Mrs Tanqueray' and supplied a hauntingly beautiful photograph of Mrs Patrick Campbell. I wrote several articles for them after that, and it was a very agreeable and useful contact.

One of my friends in the post-war period was Jonquil Anthony, the inventor and scriptwriter of that unpretending masterpiece, the precursor of 'The Archers' and 'Coronation Street', 'Mrs Dale's Diary', which ran from 1948 to 1963. This, in the width of its appeal and the hypnotic spell in which it held so many of its audience (its listening rate was said to be six million), proved what a mine of interest there is for massive audiences in a programme that presents the lives of ordinary people in walks of life similar to their own.

Jonquil's leading characters were: Dr Dale, an excellent GP, his wife Mrs Dale, their teenage son and daughter, Bob and Gwen, the daily help, the formidable Mrs Maggs, the gardener, whose name was Monument, and the cat belonging to Mrs Dale's mother Mrs Freeman, who was called Captain and had unusually large front paws. The Dales lived at Virginia Lodge, Parkwood Hill. The tone of active, ordinary existence, with just that touch of extra liveliness that expert presentation adds, proved once for all that scenes of daily life provide material to entertain the viewer and the listener which is inexhaustible.

The audience for 'The Archers' and 'Coronation Street' is, no doubt, much in excess of that of 'Mrs Dale's Diary', but the social development of the last forty years is shown by the personalia of these series compared with that of 'Mrs Dale's Diary'. The latter contained a variety of types, vividly shown, but the leading family belonged to the professional middle class. The Archers are members of the rural, agricultural society, whose characters touch a wide circumference of social interests. 'Coronation Street', I suppose, is formed on the same principal but in an urban setting; but both of them continue in the vein opened by Jonquil.

Jonquil married an actor whom she had met in the Shakespeare Company at Stratford. The marriage did not last, but as they were both interested in the stage, for a time they had a successful partnership running the little theatre in Brompton Road, The Boltons. This put on plays for fortnightly runs, and had some successful transfers to the West End.

After the marriage expired, Jonquil had a spell of other domestic interiors, in one of which she became a tenant in the house of a famous bandleader, who let out quarters in a beautiful seventeenth-century building, Cromwell House. She enjoyed the company, their liveliness and the new sphere it opened to her, but it had its drawbacks, one being that certain people were accepted by the bandleader as tenants with whom it was inconvenient, if not actually dangerous, to be under the same roof. It so happened that one of Jonquil's family married into the family of Arthur Rackham and, owing to this connection, Jonquil had inherited some of Arthur Rackham's books. Rackham had been commissioned by a publisher to illustrate a collection of fairy tales, and knowing that Edmund Dulac had illustrated a similar collection, he had bought *Edmund Dulac's Fairy Book*, to see what stories the latter had chosen to treat. This, therefore, was a book illustrated by Edmund Dulac with Arthur Rackham's signature on the flyleaf. You could have cashed it very handsomely over the counter at any book-dealer's in the Charing Cross Road.

One of Jonquil's fellow tenants in Cromwell House was a light-fingered girl, whose stay was temporary but which worked considerable havoc while it lasted. She stole an expensive type of electric iron out of a chest of drawers in another tenant's bedroom, and various desirable properties, whose loss was not noticed until she had gone. Jonquil never went anywhere without an armful of books, and her travelling library at Cromwell House had included *Edmund Dulac's Fairy Book*. It is a well-known fact about thieves that irrespective of any background knowledge, they have a sixth sense which tells them what is worth stealing. *Edmund Dulac's Fairy Book*, alas, came under this heading.

I came to understand how unremittingly active Jonquil's past life had been, in writing of all kinds, but chiefly in biographical sketches or build-ups for the BBC. (She wrote, in all, 4,000 scripts for them.) So often, if a character or place came up in conversation, she would say: 'Yes, I did a feature on that once.' Meantime, in spite of overlaying claims and distractions, the work on 'Mrs Dale's Diary' went on and on. I do not know how many times a week it played, but Jonquil headed a team of four. They met to pool suggestions for the coming instalments and decided among them which episodes should fall to the lot of each. At last there came one occasion when, by extraordinary bad luck, it happened that each of the three was incapacitated, and Jonquil was left to turn out all four scripts instead of one. The situation was considered of such desperate urgency by the BBC that they consulted the doctor who was the Corporation's usual medical adviser. He said to them: 'I can give her something that'll keep her going for twenty-four hours, but after that, she'll be on the floor.' Jonquil accepted the medication, produced all four scripts and handed them in on time. What no one, in spite of the doctor's warning, had thought to do was to ensure that somebody was in her flat to look after her.

The next day her brother and sister-in-law were expecting her to lunch. When she did not come, her brother rang her up, and getting no reply, went across London to see what had happened. He found her, as the doctor had said she would be, unconscious on the floor.

This, I think, was the beginning of her long decline in health. I remember visiting her much later when she was under the care of two excellent nurses, a day nurse and a night nurse, but presently she recovered enough to manage with daily help. I am now truly sorry that I did not then visit her often enough to follow the course of her adventures and adversities, until she moved to a council flat in the direction of Finsbury Pavement. (One had to go through Russell Square to get to the neighbourhood.) Her flat, being on the top level, was reached either by lift or several flights of stone stairs. The outlook from her large sitting room windows was wide and bright; filled with her furniture and effects, the scene was stimulating.

Jonquil's life in this flat was the beginning of a very sad procession of time, which she bore with heroism. The management of her domestic affairs was taken over by her brother; she did not lack anything in the way of physical comfort; the dreadful trial was the rapid failing of her eyesight to the point at which she could no longer read. She had considerable consolation in the records of Speaking Books, an admirable concern. They send you catalogues of their available records, and we used to go over them with her; she always knew what novels and memoirs she would like to hear. From this cavern of shadows, her death was a glorious release. I haven't done justice to her crammed life, both professional and social, or to her striking appearance. She was tall, with a round face, a beautiful complexion and dark eyes. Though so highly professional, she had a simplicity of manner which was almost schoolgirlish, though it conveyed her authority in unmistakable tones.

Her brother kindly asked me to take something of hers as a keepsake, and I chose, out of her large collection of treasures, a lovely little oval glass box, made, I should think, for comfits, of a very solid glass, a deep amber colour. It is a perfect memento of her.

Ten

๛

As I have recounted, I met Theodora Benson when we worked together in the Ministry of Information during the last years of the war. When I first visited Theodora she was living – you might almost say was perched – in a small flat at the summit of one of those blocks of buildings that wall-in Piccadilly, the lower levels being occupied by impressive offices and grand shops. It was a romantic scene, with her family possessions stacked on window-ledges and her designer clothes on hangers behind the kitchen door. She keenly enjoyed the concentrated urban nature of the setting, the ceaseless bustle on the pavements far below, and the rising hum that you would hear when you stopped talking; but she was obviously in frail health and when the lease of these premises expired she was urged, I believe by the Radcliffes, to find something of a rather healthier aspect.

As I was living in Downshire Hill she had got to know the street, and finding a house, No.10, she bought it. No.10 was of the same period as mine but much larger and had been 'made over' into two flats above the spacious ground-floor rooms. She kept two maids, but she herself attended to the garden. She also kept hens; but these conditions of healthy living did not reconcile her to being out of central London, and after a rather hectic interval she moved back into the metropolitan area. She was a most charming neighbour while she was there, but we did not often see each other, our life-styles were so different. Hers was like that of those exotic lilies that flourish best at night. Four a.m. was her normal time for going to bed, and she always took a sleeping draught. I met, briefly, many people in her house whom I would not otherwise have known. One of the most interesting was Marjorie Proops, an uncannily successful journalist, whose most famous métier was 'Answers to

Correspondents'. Once I had registered her slender figure, dressed in unassuming black, and noticed her extreme quietude in social manner, treating the exhausted, overdone Theodora like a hospital nurse of exceptional insight and kindness, I made a point of reading her Answers (they were printed in several papers and magazines) and I always marvelled at their clear-sightedness and unerring accuracy of aim. None of them was addressed to any problems within my personal experience, yet I received a vitalising impulse from reading any answer that she gave to anybody.

As part of this circle, Theodora had accepted a commission from a daily paper to write one article a week on some topic of current interest to female readers, and to volunteer to answer any letters that they sent in. The former she did, with characteristic flair, but when it came to answering the letters, she had really too much else to do. The shoal of letters was first winnowed by the newspaper, and only those sent on which it needed some sort of capacity to answer. Theodora suggested to me that if I liked to do the answering, we could split the fee – five pounds to each of us; a sum, in those days, well worth my while.

The letters were mostly about poignant but ordinary crises, and determined to learn all I could about Proops's method, I at first found the work stimulating. The case I remember with real satisfaction was that of a woman of forty, working for the first time in an office, and thoroughly enjoying this opportunity of getting to know men. Unfortunately, one of these was a middle-aged fascinator of a scoundrel who borrowed, or as it turned out, took money from her, pretending an admiration, and altogether wrecking the peace of her office life which she had at first enjoyed so much. Younger and more attractive clerks were drafted in and he pursued them, though he did not borrow money from them, as they hadn't any. He still attempted to get hers, and when she said she had no more to spare, he had said, in a tone of bitter reproach, very well, then, he must go to a moneylender. No one could stop him, and I begged her, most earnestly, not to give him any more money herself; she must of course, regard all previous loans as a dead loss, but let her absolutely make up her mind that she would not lose any more. I added that her letter gave the impression of such a warm, sensible, attractive personality, it was sad to think that she, a woman with so many good years still ahead of her, should waste herself on a situation that gave her nothing in return but distress and monetary loss. I had a most rewarding answer. She wrote that she was taking my advice, that the last time he had said he would go to a money-lender, she had said: 'Well, do!' and that my letter had encouraged her so much she carried it about with her and re-read it from time to time.

This was the top-rated letter I received; at the bottom level was one which said: 'I gave him back the ring, and I told him I never wanted to see him again. Since then, I have heard nothing from him. Do you think he is no longer interested?'

After I had been engaged in this work for some months, my brother David remarked mildly on one occasion that he was not sure that all this expert opinion ought to be reaching the newspaper's readers simply for the cost of a postage stamp. I was beginning to feel somewhat worn out myself, and was much relieved when Theodora said she'd decided to end the commission, and hoped it wouldn't inconvenience me. It chimed in beautifully. I was very glad to have had the experience and the money, and also to have finished with it.

Before the war Theodora had come before the public as a novelist. She had had a *succès d'estime* with two or three novels in the pensive, débutante style. Victor Gollancz had taken to her warmly; he spoke of her as 'my Theo' and though the money she brought in cannot have been much, the acclaim, in certain circles, was considerable. She seemed always to be trembling on the verge of a flare-up of success but it did not happen. We discussed the emergence of the reportage novel, and she declared she would write one, on the profession of undertaking; it was to be called *The Undertaker's Wife*. I immediately foresaw something of morbid elegance, fit to make you shudder; reminiscent, perhaps, of Edgar Allan Poe. Theodora was in touch with a rather rakish new young publisher, who, fired by our conversation about the reportage novel, made her an offer for this unwritten work.

Theodora remembered, just in time, that every contract for a novel that you signed with Victor Gollancz gave him the first refusal of your next three. So she wrote to him explaining that it would really be to *his* advantage that she should break the contract: she wasn't a money-spinner, and this work would be quite a new departure for her, into which she by no means saw her way. She had a letter in reply which began: 'My dearest Theodora' and ended 'Ever yours, most affectionately, Victor Gollancz'; only the part in between wasn't so satisfactory. It said that the firm were most interested in this idea of her new departure, and when might they hope to receive the script? So she wrote the novel which Victor published and I read, but it featured none of the macabre elements which I had supposed would be its *raison d'être*. In fact it contained nothing at all outside the experience of the wife of any competent tradesman, in grocery, or hardware or stationery. Victor telephoned me some time afterwards, saying: 'What *is* the matter with her? Do you know? If I knew, I think I could help her.' Alas, I had to say I didn't know. (So kind, so ready to help anybody, but for herself, she could do nothing.) When she was not listening with luminous attention, or making some salty, sparkling comment, she relapsed into that sphere which reminded you of the arrival of Odysseus at the darkened land of the Cimmereans: 'to the limits of the world, to the deep-flowing Oceanus'.

You would have said Theodora had everything: looks, money, social success, professional success. I think, now, that her condition was partly accounted for by her taking too much of that sleeping draught, and also, one might hazard, that the thing she wanted most was the thing she hadn't got. No one who saw a good deal of her could fail to realise that she was surrounded by men, either interested in her, or on the verge of becoming interested; answering her office telephone while she was out the room was enough to tell you that. If she wanted to be married, she could have been; but what she longed for, I believe, was to be united to somebody in a *grande passion*. When she was a girl, she had had exactly this; but her attempts to keep it secret from her family had failed, and the man not being considered eligible, her mother had broken off the affair with characteristic energy. Theodora spoke of it to me only in the briefest terms, but I sensed how painful it must have been. In the perspective of time, one can see that it had been more than that – it had been fatal. But I did not understand this till long afterwards, and if I had, she already inspired so much sympathy and affection in so many people, what more could I have offered?

She died from an attack of pneumonia while she was staying with the Radcliffes in their country house. Lord Radcliffe telephoned me and asked me to write her obituary for *The Times*. When I began to say I did not think I could, his request became a command, so I agreed to do my best.

As I was thinking about her in a spell of concentration, by a sudden inspiration there came into my mind the reason why she had never achieved the literary success that was expected for her. It was that she gave so much precious time, and still more precious nervous energy, to listening to other people's troubles, supporting and encouraging them. If someone had charged her with this, and told her to shut herself up until whatever book she was working on was finished, her answer, I think, would have been: 'Am I to say I won't live, because I want to write?'

Elizabeth Bowen once said to me that I was the least irritating person she knew. Seeing how very highly strung she was, this was gratifying. She was indeed taut to a degree, but, unusually, she combined this quality with a physique that could almost be called robust: tall, strong and graceful. She had an innate elegance; her quiet, beautiful, expensive clothes expressed it, and the force of her conversational idiom, altogether simple and natural (its charm enhanced by a slight, intermittent stammer), owed nothing to slang or jargon: to what are now called 'buzz words'. She was highly sexed herself, and attractive to men. You could scarcely explain this impression since her behaviour was always decorous, but she bore about her the aroma of passionate experiences. Mollie Keane in a little recollection-piece about her, given on the air, said that a characteristic memory of her was that when you went to a party, you found all the men you would most like to talk to standing round Elizabeth.

Elizabeth had, like any able novelist, an acutely sensitive ear for the idiom of conversation, and she was in touch with many social strata on which to draw: the Anglo-Irish society into which she was born, the distinguished level of Oxford society in which she and her husband, Alan Cameron, had lived when he was the Education Officer for the district, and the height of *réclame* in London literary society.

One of the charms of her conversation was spontaneous witticism. The last time she was in my house I had given a small party for her, and one of the young men had asked if he might bring his girl. I said 'Do!' but when they arrived it turned out she couldn't speak a word of English. She was, however, so pretty and full of enjoyment that some young men rushed forward and managed to talk to her – in what language, I don't remember. When everyone had gone, I said to Elizabeth: 'I'm a poor hostess – I ought to have worked harder for her.' Elizabeth said: 'Don't give it a thought! Girls like that are brought along at owner's risk.'

She spent that night at Downshire Hill, and I have still the letter she wrote to me afterwards. She had been reading my novel *Dr Gully* in bed. She wrote: 'The hours up there in my room in your house will be forever tied up with Dr Gully. When I reached the last page in my bed there, I lay for some time with my eyes shut, "stretched for dead", as they say in Ireland.' This was one of the last times I saw her.

After the death of Virginia Woolf, Elizabeth was undoubtedly the most celebrated woman-writer of the day. This meant that she was sometimes the target for spiteful remarks from some other women writers, but her generosity and kindness, as well as her charm, made her generally very much liked. One of her best novels, in my view, was *The Last September*, which after a brilliantly satiric picture of Irish landowners and the conceited and ignorant women who accompanied husbands serving in the Black and Tans, sent over to protect the landowners from the IRA, culminates in a horrifying picture of the Great House set alight and burning to the ground.

Elizabeth's own house, Bowen's Court in County Cork, was a beautiful and mournful spectacle. It was a mid-eighteenth-century building, with the spacious, lofty rooms and large-paned sash-windows of the era, but apart from the bedrooms, the dining room and the drawing room, it was so scantily furnished as to seem almost uninhabited. One afternoon, when I had been for a walk with her in Regent's Park and we had come back to tea in Clarence Gate, she picked up a pile of letters from the hall table and brought them with her into the drawing room. She said: 'I sometimes wonder what my feelings would be if one of these letter were to say that Bowen's Court was actually burned down.'

Though her roots were in Ireland, her chosen scene was Clarence Gate, the short row of houses at right angles to the end of Clarence Terrace. The enormous sash-windows, pouring in light, the lovely pieces of Regency furniture, whose presence in these rooms perhaps partly accounted for the bareness of some in Bowen's Court, made a groundwork of timeless elegance and beauty and the natural setting for one of her most successful novels, *The Death of the Heart*.

Victor Gollancz, allured, naturally, by her celebrity, had said 'Write a novel for me!' And this was it. Victor did well with it from the commercial angle, but the cold, clear light in which it was steeped I think almost petrified him. Elizabeth told me the story of her celebratory, post-publishing lunch with him; it is hard to credit, and yet it is true. Throughout the meal he did not refer once to *The Death of the Heart*. As they were parting, he said, gruffly, he would be glad to hear about her next novel. Victor subsequently said to me that when his wife asked him about the lunch, and what Elizabeth was like, he had described her as 'a brilliant baby'. Her next novel, *The Heat of the Day*, went to Cape. Many people think this is her best work, and one can see why. The long-drawn-out, torturing uneasiness of the situation, in which the lover is, at last, revealed as a spy, is oppressively gripping, while his family, in particular the ludicrous figure of his sister, are perhaps the strongest comic turns in the whole body of Elizabeth's work. I think it is not, now, indiscreet to mention Elizabeth had a love affair of an absorbing kind with a man whose official duties kept him, for long spells, out of the country. During one of these, he married. For the novel, the hero was revealed as a traitor.

My own favourite, *The Death of the Heart*, contains, among other features of high interest, in the hero-villain a portrait of Goronwy Rees. On reading it, the latter declared that he would bring an action for libel; but Alan Cameron told Elizabeth not to be distressed; he had consulted their solicitor, who had promised him that if Goronwy Rees went into the witness-box to claim that 'Eddie' was an unmistakable portrait of himself, he, the solicitor, would be prepared to bring forward two other young men, each of whom would assert that 'Eddie' was he himself, to the life. No more was heard of any proposed action on the part of Mr Rees in this connection.

Lord David Cecil's admiration for Elizabeth, and their mutual affection, were well-known; each of them was happily married – a state to which the friendship did no injury. Lord David was for some years the President of the Jane Austen Society and he invited Elizabeth to give the address at the Annual General Meeting of 1969. In this she said: 'Returning to those novels of hers, again and again, we feel more, rather than less, involved in them, as our lives go on ... at each re-reading we are the more struck by instances of her uncanny perception.' Lord David had introduced her as the speaker in terms of the highest praise. When she finished, instead of the usual words of appreciation and thanks, he merely made a gesture, turning his hands outwards, and exclaimed in triumph: 'There!'

One Christmas when I was asked to dinner at Clarence Gate, I arrived before Elizabeth had come down. In the drawing room by myself, I was enthralled by the glorious display of Christmas cards on the chimneypiece. One was particularly beautiful: a Regency print bordered with gilt foil. I chose to think it was not wrong to read the message on a Christmas card publicly displayed. It said, merely, 'Forget-me-not, David.'

In the collection of articles she called *Afterthought*, Elizabeth described the pressures of this age: 'Our century, as it takes its maddening course, seems barely habitable to humans. We have to learn to survive while we learn to write.' Her sketch (in the volume *The Demon Lover*) 'Mysterious Kor' is an uncannily vivid description of a brilliant moonlight night among the cliffs of white terraces in Regent's Park, during the war when all street lighting was off and the light from house-windows screened. 'Full moonlight drenched the city and searched it out … the moon … blazed in windows that looked that way.' A soldier and his girl are walking by moonlight in the park, and she says she has never forgotten the poem:

> Mysterious Kor, thy walls forsaken stand,
> Thy lonely towers beneath a lonely moon…

I, alas, have never been able to find it; I did not read the description while I could have asked her where it was.

At the end of the war my brother David, having failed in his attempt to enter the Services, had an introduction from Elizabeth Bowen which resulted in his being accepted as a member of the Friends' Overseas Relief Service Delegation. His detachment was sent to Warsaw. He told me almost nothing of the conditions they discovered in the abandoned concentration camps, except that one included instruments of torture, and that a stout Nazi official went down on his knees, almost blubbering, as he assured them he had never seen these objects before. The details of the inexpressibly horrible conditions began, after a time, to make David feel faint and he went outside to sit down for a few minutes in the open air. Then he had what, in retrospect, he thought a very interesting experience. Instead of being conscious of a bright morning prospect, it looked to him as if everywhere around him had become dark. He wondered, afterwards, if this might be a natural reaction to contemplating horrors, and if so, if it were part of the explanation of what three of the four Gospels say, that at the Crucifixion there was darkness over the land.

When he came back to London, he was taken into partnership by the firm of solicitors then called Walters and Hart. The senior partner, known as 'Boy' Hart, was a cheerful man, of intense interests, both professional and aesthetic. He had established the firm in one of the beautiful Regency houses in Mansfield Street. Most solicitors, dealing with such a house, would have cut up the ballroom into office space. Boy Hart kept it as it was; that, and the lovely, soaring staircase and the marble-paved entrance hall made, for him, an enjoyable background for the success of a thriving business. One of the senior partners, Sir Dingwall Bateson, might well have been reckoned among the elegant fixtures of Walters and Hart; he had been required to scan the evidence as to which of the peers had the right to carry the orb at the Queen's coronation. He was recounting his researches to David, and broke off to say: 'Now listen to this, David, it ought to interest you.' He could hardly have been speaking to anyone whom it would have interested more, but my brother, who was, I believe, exceptionally perceptive and keen-witted, did appear occasionally to be thinking about something else. It struck me as odd that Mr Balgarnie, the senior classics master at The Leys (one of his pupils, James Hilton, later portrayed him vividly as Mr Chips in a number of novels), and my brother's housemaster, should once have said to him: 'Jenkins, do you *ever* listen to anything that's said to you?' David, in relating this, said that Mr Balgarnie was always disappointed in him; Romilly had been a favourite pupil, absorbed in Greek and Latin, while he himself had been equally devoted to history and English literature. Mr Balgarnie's friendship with Romilly had been life-long. James Hilton's final work in the Mr Chips series was *Goodbye, Mr Chips*. Of this, Mr Balgarnie had said, in a letter to Romilly: 'I am glad to say goodbye to Mr Chips who, first and last, has caused me much suffering.'

David now had a standing invitation to Sunday lunch at Downshire Hill unless one of us was away for the weekend. We had both become very friendly with Paul Stephenson, whom originally I got to know because he was a cousin of my close friend Ann Sitwell. Paul had had a varied career, beginning as an actor, then becoming one of the drama directors at the BBC. On one occasion he asked me to read aloud a 'talk' he'd written. When I had finished, he said: 'I hadn't realised how well I'd done it till I heard you reading it.' One of his BBC features had been the production of Hugh Ross Williamson's series entitled 'Historical Whodunits', recounting and supplying explanations of fourteen mysterious deaths of characters in history. Most of Mr Ross Williamson's accounts were somewhat perverse, with the exception of his version of the death of Sir Edmund Berry Godfrey, which was widely acclaimed as being not only original but incontestable.

Paul had remarkable sympathy and insight, and when he became a prison visitor he would talk so perceptively of problems and perplexities in the lives of prisoners you almost felt that you had experienced these difficulties yourself. David enjoyed his company greatly; one could see that in their friendship each supplied something the other had not acquired. Paul always came to us for one of the meals over the Bank Holiday weekends, either on Saturday, Sunday or Monday. As the time drew near, David would say: 'Have you asked Paul?' If I said 'Not yet, but I'm going to', he would say 'Don't leave it too late.'

On one of these occasions Paul arrived in a raincoat at which we exclaimed in admiration: gun metal waterproof silk, with a small waterproof cape over each shoulder, and such *couture*! To our amazement, it turned out that he had acquired this garment at a knockdown price from Wakefield Gaol. A quantity of them had been ordered for the warders but, surprisingly, the warders, as a whole, hadn't cared for them; the prison authorities found they had several left on their hands and had been glad to get anybody to take one.

I never asked Paul for details, but I feel it was characteristic of him that he should have gone up to Yorkshire to visit Wakefield Gaol. He never grudged a visit, however distant, to someone whom he had once befriended, but who had relapsed and incurred another sentence. Once we were talking about a young man known to both of us who had been so stimulated by Paul's account of his experiences, he thought he would like to visit prisoners himself: 'provided', he said 'they were ones worth helping; I wouldn't want to waste my time.' Paul said to me: 'I knew then he'd never be any good at it.'

Paul died in June 1985, his death was very sudden. His memorial service was held in St James's Church, Islington. The front pews were filled with tough-looking young men, accompanied by girls; many of them weeping. It reminded one of having read that though Dr Johnson had composed a stately epitaph on Goldsmith which was put up in Westminster Abbey, Goldsmith's most poignant memorial was the wailing of the poor Irish on the stairs outside his lodging.

Eleven

In the mid-1960s I wrote two novels in succession, *Brightness* and *Honey*, both of which contained for me some of the most satisfying novel writing I ever did. The first hinged on the report of the trial for manslaughter of a Cambridge undergraduate, the son of a wealthy family, who owned a racing car and who used to say that motoring 'didn't amuse' him unless he were driving at eighty miles an hour. He was speeding when one of his tyres burst; the car, out of control, mounted the pavement, killed two elderly women walking there, and would have killed an undergraduate if the young man hadn't tumbled into a ditch. I thought: suppose he had killed the undergraduate. I made this imagined tragedy the climax of a story which I formed on the character of one of my uncles, Romilly Ingram, whom I have already mentioned, who went out as a missionary to India and died of smallpox at the age of twenty-three. This was before I was born, but his character had left such an impression on his large family, I felt as if I had known him. Victor Gollancz said the book had moved him profoundly, and I had an unusual number of letters about it.

The other novel I had wanted to call 'Venus and Adonis'. It was about the attempted seduction of a schoolboy by an extremely attractive woman who was obsessed with anxiety because she had begun to notice that though she made as many conquests as ever, they were never, now, of very young men. The background of the story was the boys' school at which the hero and his friend both attended. I found that with my upbringing and my ten years' teaching experience in a co-educational school, I had the sort of experience that comes into your mind without your calling it: experience not of fact or routine, but of professional attitudes. I think the two boys were successfully brought off, but the character that people seemed to like most was a composition of several schoolmasters I had known; men who had rather be in the teaching profession than any other, a blend of experience and freshness, calm but responsive. By the time I had handed in the text, Victor had died – a desperately sad loss for a wide number of people. The firm said that my title must be altered; though their readers would be familiar with the idea of Venus, they wouldn't see the force of Adonis. So they entitled it *Honey*, the name of the disreputable heroine, which was suitable enough.

After the death of Victor Gollancz, the firm did not continue his practice of signing you up for your next three books; so when my friend Raleigh Trevelyan, who was then with Michael Joseph, asked me what book I was working on and liked the answer, I was free to commit it to him. It was about the Bravo Case of 1876, in which, in my view, by far the most interesting figure was not the victim, Charles Bravo, or his beautiful but selfish wife, Florence, but Dr James Gully, then famous all over England – even attracting patients from America and Russia as having, with Dr Wilson, instituted the 'water cure' at Malvern.

I had first written about the Bravo Case in my book of sketches entitled *Six Criminal Women*. I subsequently reverted to it when the *Sunday Express* invited me to analyse the Bravo Affair as a contribution to a series on Unsolved Mysteries, an opportunity I owed to Agatha Christie who was first asked by the *Sunday Express* to write up the case. She replied that she was too busy, but that she hoped they could find someone to take it on as the story was of such interest.

I subsequently met Agatha Christie at a lunch party at All Souls given by Dr Rowse. When I saw her, it struck me that she was the most elegantly dressed elderly woman I had ever seen. At that time it was possible to be fashionable in skirts of reasonable length; her high-necked, long-sleeved dress was mole-coloured, and she wore a sweeping, cavalier-like felt hat of the same colour; her court shoes were black with marcasite buckles; on one shoulder was a superb diamond brooch, which took the eye without blinding it. She was so charming, so quiet, so interesting, while saying very little. At Dr Rowse's lunch parties, some of the college plate was arranged as a centrepiece. At one point in this meal, I saw her stretch out her hand and draw a silver flagon towards her, turning it upside-down to examine the assay-mark, then sliding it gently back again. I read afterwards that antique silver was one of her interests. Her detective thrillers have always seemed to me the most absorbing in the whole of this genre. Other writers produced more interesting characters, a more fashionable slant, but for me (one of multitudes), that point in her book which you reach just before you are told the answer exerts a tension of which no other writer is capable.

When I wrote my version of the Bravo Case in the book which had come out in 1949, I made a serious mistake in my proposed solution of the mystery. It is only right to say that the idea was widely accepted at the time and had the authority of Sir John Hall, in his book *The Bravo Mystery and Other Cases* (Bodley Head, 1925). This view was that Mrs Bravo's companion, Mrs Cox, with the former's compliance, had done Charles Bravo to death with a dose of antimony, otherwise known as tartar emetic. Charles Bravo was a self-seeking young man, who was genuinely fond of his wife, Florence, but even more attached to her fortune. He could not touch the money which was settled on her, but he had insisted that all her property should be left out of the marriage settlement, so that furniture, plate, jewellery, horses, carriages, chattels of every description, and the lease of her house, The Priory, at Balham, all became his the moment the marriage ceremony was completed.

Nevertheless, Charles Bravo was always thinking of how his wife's spending could be curtailed: when he had cut down the expenses of her garden, and arranged that her personal maid should be dismissed, it occurred to him that with their large domestic staff they could do without the somewhat expensive services of Mrs Cox. But before this retrenchment could be effected, one evening, on going to bed, he was seized with stomach pains and vomiting, and though his wife showed every sign of distress and summoned six doctors, one after the other, as well as his parents and her own, he died five days later, and the long legal process, with questions in Parliament and nationwide newspaper coverage, involved Dr Gully, a fashionable physician and the owner of an enormous practice at Malvern in the mid-nineteenth century. Although married to a much older woman (from whom he was living apart), Dr Gully had become Florence's lover during her first widowhood and their affair was passionate, cooling only under the stress of Florence's increasingly erratic behaviour. Dr Gully had never seen Florence since her subsequent marriage to Charles Bravo; but the Bravos' coachman, George Griffith, had been Dr Gully's coachman at Malvern, and though Dr Gully did not want his horses treated with any lotion except cold water, Griffith thought he knew better and had bought, in Dr Gully's name, some ounces of tartar emetic from a Malvern chemist. The remains of this he had brought to The Priory, and when Charles Bravo dismissed him, he left it behind him in the coachman's harness room.

Florence Bravo was still suffering from the prostrating effects of two miscarriages and when her husband showed signs of wanting to return to her bed, she employed, I now believe, one of the few contraceptive devices known to the time, that of administering an emetic, which provided a temporary defence. This explanation has been supported by my friend Dr Laetitia Fairfield who was once the Secretary of the Medico-Legal Society. Mrs Bravo had drunk a great deal of wine at dinner that evening, and had sent for more wine after she had gone upstairs. It was known that Charles Bravo always drank off the contents of the water bottle on his washstand before going to bed; Mrs Bravo, we believe, meant to administer an emetic dose in this water bottle. Five grains of tartar emetic would have produced vomiting, ten grains would be lethal. The postmortem on Charles Bravo showed that he had swallowed thirty. This preposterous overdose seems to speak of a woman too drunk to know what she was doing, not of the competent and cautious Mrs Cox.

The legal proceedings involved two inquests: in the first, the jury found that Bravo had died from the effects of poison, but that there was not sufficient evidence to show under what circumstances it came into his body – thus leaving open the possibility of suicide. This verdict provoked a wave of public speculation, as well as castigation by the press of the hasty way the inquest had been conducted. At the request of the Attorney-General, the verdict was quashed and a second inquest was held, at which Dr Gully was obliged to give evidence about his previous 'criminal intimacy' with Florence Ricardo, including the fact that he had performed an abortion on her. The second verdict was that Bravo had been murdered by the administration of poison 'but that there was not sufficient evidence to fix the guilt upon any person or persons'. With this inconclusive result, the legal process was closed, although unbridled speculation in the press went on for many months. There was no evidence to implicate Dr Gully in Charles Bravo's death, either directly or indirectly, but his reputation, both personal and professional, was destroyed.

I had become obsessed by the Bravo story, simply because I found the personality of Dr Gully of such interest. He had a devoted following of patients and a reputation for wisdom and perspicacity stretching well beyond Malvern. He was indeed unlucky in his infatuation for Florence Ricardo, as she then was. To read everything available about Dr Gully, to visit Malvern time and again and see so much of it untouched since his own day – especially, on Wells Road, the two houses standing beside each other, Holyrood House and Newby House, in which he housed his patients – I found exciting beyond description.

Malvern at the beginning of the nineteenth century had been a hillside village. The brilliant success of Dr Gully and Dr Wilson as practisers of hydrotherapy had changed it into a thriving little town. In a country district the buildings of 1830 and 1840 retained, in their pro-Gothic style, some of the late eighteenth-century gracefulness, not yet hardened into the over-elaboration and heaviness of Victorian Gothic. Dr Gully's two houses (now forming the Tudor

Hotel) had their front entrances on Wells Road, but originally these had been back entrances, while on the other side of the houses long flights of steps led down to Abbey Road. The front entrance of the Tudor Hotel has now been modernised, but inside it, intact, is the back entrance to Newby House. The door is jewel-like; the square panes of thickly frosted glass are framed in oblong slips of coloured glass: crimson, violet, blue. Inside the Tudor Hotel almost all the original construction remains untouched, staircases, banisters, windows, doors. One feature created by Dr Gully found its way into the histories of the water cure: on mezzanine level, the two houses were joined by a bridge, one side of it all windows, over-looking the splendid view. Dr Gully had decided that, except on specified social occasions, male and female patients should be kept separated, and this bridge was known to the local wits as the 'Bridge of Sighs'. One passed over it to get to the hotel dining room.

Dr Gully published two books, for which the material was drawn from his professional experience: *The Water Cure in Chronic Disease* (1846) and *The Water Cure in Acute Disease* (1864). The latter is the more interesting to the non-medical reader, as it contains an abundance of social comment. On my second visit to Malvern I was roaming round the shelves of the public library in Graham Road, when I came across *The Water Cure in Acute Disease*, and written inside the cover – 'With the compliments of the Author'. Imagine! I went to one of the pleasant ladies at the desk and, showing her the book, I told her how interesting and valuable it was. She was new to the position and had not yet heard of Dr Gully. When I explained who and what he was, she thanked me warmly for telling her. On a subsequent visit I found that this book and some others of local interest were in a glass-fronted cupboard in what had now been labelled 'The Malvern Room'.

I have recounted earlier that I was thought by some people to have committed an ignoble fraud when I published my novel *Harriet* in 1934, as it was a story of actual happenings. The literary climate had changed so much since then that no one raised any objection when I brought out *Dr Gully* in 1972, with the exception

of the late Phyllis Mann of Malvern who, as a very painstaking
local historian, had steeped herself in the town's development and
the history of its inhabitants so far as they were contemporary with
Dr Gully. It was a work of love; she plainly had a respect for him
amounting to hero-worship, as I had. Unfortunately she had not
the capacity to make the reader share her interest; the posthumously published pamphlet was entitled, merely, *Collections for a
Life and Background of James Mauby Gully M.D* (1983) and its
contents were not liable to arouse interest in any one who was not
taken by the subject already. They did not relate any episodes
conveying the idea of Dr Gully's personality, or of that aspect which
people mean when they speak of 'a born doctor'. So far as his
connection with the Bravo case was concerned, Miss Mann's treatment of this was scanty to a degree; and while very rightly exempt-
ing him from any connection with Charles Bravo's death, she had
not, in this posthumous fragment, given any idea of the extraordinary interest the case aroused, or of the *mise-en-scène*. She rejected
with scorn that mine of contemporary information, *The Bravo
Case*, published in seven parts by *The Daily Telegraph* of the day,
which gave verbatim reports of the second inquest, and brief
biographical accounts of the protagonists. Particularly interesting
are the drawings of the persons concerned and some sketches,
notably the densely crowded billiard room at the Bedford Hotel,
with Mrs Cox giving evidence.

However, Miss Mann was celebrated in Malvern as a person of
literary distinction; she was recorded as having written on Shelley,
Keats, Lamb and Mrs Browning, though she had not published
anything, as I found when I looked for works by her in the catalogue of the British Library. Although I had paid so many visits to
Malvern, I had never heard of her until the last of these when I was
told that she was highly indignant with me, and one can see why.
Her posthumous collection is so scanty and so dry, it is impossible
to imagine how she would have made it into a publishable work,
but she regarded herself, and was regarded by her friends, as the
supreme authority on Dr Gully and his career. Then my book was

published, and this was too hard for her to bear with equanimity. I would have dearly liked to make the book a 'straight' biography, but without medical background you cannot write the life of a doctor. So I wrote it as a 'period' novel; but I researched it as thoroughly as if I had been writing a biography. Miss Mann's natural reaction was to point out various instances in which I had had to eke out my ignorance with imagination – the Christian name of Mrs Bravo's sister, the family connections of Dr Gully's butler, Pritchard, the links, the scenes and conversations which I had been obliged to invent to carry on the story. What I did not, and do not, understand is why every time she referred to my book, she called it 'the novel' in inverted commas. What would she have wanted me to call it? To say it was a biography was, on the face of it, impossible, since it contained passages of invention.

Miss Mann, I see, died in 1982. She would, I dare say, have rejected any offers of communication with me, but I am sorry I had no opportunity of giving her information that I am sure would have pleased her. My late friend Judge H. C Leon (who wrote under the name of Henry Cecil) was a member of the Garrick Club, as was Dr Gully. The latter's name had been removed from the General Medical Council, but in the most merciful manner under 'Address no longer known'. However, contrary to the statement in *The Dictionary of National Biography*, that his name had been removed from the learned societies to which he had belonged, he had not been deprived of his Fellowship of the Royal Medical and Chirurgical Society of London, nor of the Royal Physical Society of Edinburgh; nor, as Harry Leon found out from the records of the club, had he been asked to resign from the Garrick. He was on record as a member of this club till his death. That, I am sure, would have pleased Miss Mann very much. I wish, now, I could have told her.

It was exciting when the BBC decided to make a three-part television serial on the Bravo case with Robert Harris in the lead as Dr Gully. Robert became one of the most interesting and closest friends of my later life. He was generally called Bobby, but when he telephoned me, he always said 'Robert here', so I called him Robert. He lived with his friend Norman Wright, the drama producer I have mentioned in connection with the BBC's performance of my play *King Monmouth*. One was always keyed up by Robert: to be sympathetic, intelligent, good value; but Norman left one nothing to do, he was immediately genial, infectiously amusing, always listening keenly and giving sound advice. Visits to them were a delight. Norman was a superb cook, not merely a very good one; the conversation there was stimulating, hilarious. Friendship with them made one understand that homosexual men can have not only affection for women, but even a degree of romantic affection.

I heard through a friendly mediator that the BBC had decided they were not going to use my book *Dr Gully*, in fact they did not want me anywhere near the place! Their scriptwriter was an authority – in fact *the* authority on the case; he had not read my book and did not intend to. As the matter was 'in the public domain' there was no question of copyright unless he had, in part, used my book, and it was asserted that he had not; but something amusing came from this affair. When the script was sent to Robert he felt that some of his lines were altogether unsatisfactory. He said to me on the telephone: 'Come round and let us go through it and try to make it sayable.' So after one of Norman's dinners, Robert and I sat side by side on the sofa and he pointed out the lines he didn't approve of; I suggested alterations, and he wrote them in.

Florence Bravo's family, whose name was Campbell, were wealthy Australian sheep-farmers, who had retired to England and settled themselves in a beautiful Georgian house, Buscot Park in Berkshire. The house was now owned by Lord Faringdon, a friend of Robert's who, when filming was finished, asked us all to a lunch party. Afterwards we walked across to the small Buscot church. Florence is buried on the left side of the south porch; the grave is marked only by a block of white marble, enclosed in a narrow white marble border. It does not bear Florence's name, only that of one of her brothers, Herbert, and her aunt, Margaret Campbell. The BBC's scriptwriter no doubt was the one who identified the tomb for them as that of Florence, but when the BBC version of the story was screened, I was sent a letter written by someone recounting a conversation with an old woman whose father, when a young man, had helped to carry Florence's coffin to the grave in 1878. After the inquest on Charles Bravo, she had separated from her family and retired to a house in Southsea, where, on 21 September, the poor creature drank herself to death. The old woman's father remembered that the burial was carried out at 5 a.m; in September it must have been dark at that hour. Her father and mother were not buried in the grave; they had themselves interred in the churchyard of the neighbouring village of Easton Hastings. The last shot of the film showed Robert standing beside that grave, looking down at the marble slab with a face expressing tenderness, remorse and a trace of ironic humour.

The whole cast and the production were admirable. For the first time in my life I hired a television set at the lowest possible rate to cover the fortnight during which the three parts of the serial were shown. When the licence I had paid for ran out and I had returned the set to the rental firm, the Licensing Authority simply could not believe that I had sent back the set after such a brief tenure; they sent me notice after notice, of an increasingly threatening kind, and finally one assuring me that when their special van was driven up to my front gate, the machinery in it would detect the presence of television in my house. At this I wrote in courteous style, asking them to make their own appointment to call at 8 Downshire Hill, when they could examine every cupboard and wardrobe in the house to discover any concealed television set. After this, I heard no more.

Twelve

୫

A. L. Rowse had a devouring interest in the history of any age or place, but his ruling passion was the Elizabethan age in England, covering the life and works of Shakespeare. Of his great number of published works, I suppose the most famous are *The England of Elizabeth* and *William Shakespeare: a Biography*. One of the charms of his writing was his unusually acute visual sense. I had always thought my own was keen, but on one of my visits to Oxford he took me into the chapel of Exeter College. They have there the original of the familiar painting by Burne-Jones of the Virgin seated under a little thatched shelter, with her baby on her knee. In the background an angel stands protectively, as I thought, but ALR exclaimed: 'Look! Do you see, he's hovering.' So he is: the feet are stretched, as if on tiptoe, not actually touching the ground.

Macaulay told Acton, then a young historian, that if you are writing about a place of historical interest, you must go to see it, or what remains of it. (One wonders whether The Glen of Weeping was Macaulay's own name for Glencoe: it is said not to be found in any contemporary guide books.) Rowse adopted this maxim fervently; his faculty for seeing extended to an all-round view of the human subject. Marlowe and Shakespeare were, however uneasily, friends of each other, both being protégés of Lord Southampton. Marlowe had been manslaughtered in a tavern brawl in 1595; his poem *Hero and Leander* was posthumously published in 1596. Shakespeare wrote *Romeo and Juliet* in 1597, and *As You Like It* in 1599 and quoted lines from Marlowe in both of them; having, as Rowse says, 'retained them in his actor's memory'. Another example, among many, of this perception is Rowse's description of Leander's hair, looking like the Golden Fleece and 'never shorn'. As

Rowse says, this is not how young Greek men wore their hair, but it is how Lord Southampton wore his; and he reproduces in his book, *Southampton,* three portraits showing Southampton's hair falling below his shoulders.

So much of his research told you what you had always wanted to know. After the defeat of her army at Langside in 1568, Mary Queen of Scots fled into England and wrote to Queen Elizabeth demanding assistance of all kinds, including clothes. The Spanish Ambassador 'had heard' that Elizabeth had sent her a parcel containing 'two worn-out chemises and a pair of shoes'. Mary's own report to the French court was: 'The Queen of England has sent me a little linen', a gift which, however inadequate, does not correspond with what the Spanish Ambassador 'had heard', and Rowse quotes items from 'the book of Warrants from the Great Wardrobe' of 1568: 'for the Queen of Scots, sixteen yards of black velvet, sixteen yards of black satin, ten yards of black taffeta'. Since the Spanish Ambassador's version of this episode has passed into history, one wishes that the Doctor, on this occasion, had not shown the characteristic masculine indifference to the details of female dress, but had quoted these items from the Great Wardrobe Warrants, with special emphasis.

Among the many details of extreme interest in his *William Shakespeare* is his noting that the local records show that, in 1589, at Tiddington, in the neighbourhood of Stratford, Katherine Hamlet was found drowned in the Avon. Twelve years later Shakespeare was writing *Hamlet:* 'The name Hamlet would be enough to bring it all back ... there had to be a coroner's inquest in Stratford, for the jury to decide whether the death were accident or suicide.' One of the gravediggers at work on Ophelia's grave says to the other: 'If this had not been a gentlewoman, she should have been buried out o' Christian burial.'

After *Dr Gully* Raleigh Trevelyan wanted me to do another book for Michael Joseph. I hadn't any idea in my head for one till he suggested King Arthur. Arthur to me, then, was merely a lofty, glamorous, indistinct figure of one's childhood, but as Raleigh spoke, various impressions began to collect in my mind, creating an impulse.

The most powerful of these was the enthusiasm of Dr Rowse. He and Raleigh were firm friends and each of them had a house in Cornwall. The Doctor's was at St Austell. He invited me there in 1974, suggesting that I should spend half the week with him and the other half at the house Raleigh shared with his friend Raoul Balin.

As I have said, it was the Doctor who gave me my first insight into the story of Arthur: that he was not a king but a highly successful cavalry commander of Romano-British origin, with extraordinary charisma and powers of military leadership. Julius Caesar had begun the conquest of Britain in 40 BC, but the demands of the Roman empire made it impossible for him to hold down the conquest, which was completed by the Emperor Claudius in AD 43. The instrument of his power was the Roman legion, whose armour, cavalry and discipline were inherited by Arthur and used with tremendous force against the hordes of Saxon invaders who entered on the south-east coast and began a hideous wreckage of the civilisation the Romans had left behind. Arthur's resistance, even with mounted soldiers, could not turn out the Saxons, unmounted though these were; but it checked their advance into the south-west. The early Saxon reputation for savage cruelty and ruthless destruction was so dreadful that the leader who was victorious against them became a national hero; he was a saviour, and for centuries many people refused to believe that he was dead (a belief strengthened by the fact that no one could say where he had been buried) and they remained longing for, and expecting, his return.

The growth and the invasive power of the myth were of course only possible through centuries of an unmechanised civilisation, in a land of forests, of rivers spanned by only a few bridges, and with a very small population. That the myth became so powerful and so lasting, with Arthur transformed into a king who had a magician for his adviser, and who, yet, established a court which practised all the arts and refinements of medieval chivalry, is not only of historical interest, in the matter of what details may be accepted as founded on fact. It also speaks for the intense quality of the English imagination, since the growth of a myth depends not only on the skill of the storyteller, but also on the receptiveness of the listeners. The earliest form of the transmogrification of the Romano-British cavalry leader into the immortal king was a version of the collection of local legends made by the twelfth-century Welsh monk, Geoffrey of Monmouth. Geoffrey was the first to publish the story that Arthur was conceived and born in the castle of Tintagel, on the rocky island off the west coast of Cornwall; this was once joined to the mainland, but since the nineteenth century the connecting ridge of rock had been eroded away. The island still bears traces of the ruins of a monastery.

The Doctor drove me from his house in St Austell to Tintagel, a distance almost half the length of the county of Cornwall. The sight and sound of the pounding waves of the Bristol Channel, surging up the small, stony beaches and against the enormous rocks, makes the scene as exciting as the legend.

During my three days' visit at St Austell, we sat up talking and arguing till very late at night. In the course of these vigorous and disputatious conversations, the Doctor said: 'It would never do for us to see too much of each other: we should kill each other.' There was, however, no question of any killing. The only disturbing element I ever received from his society (apart from the fear that one might, unknowingly, set off a shattering explosion) was that his remarkable success, both in England and America, and his considerable wealth, seemed to have no mellowing effect on his nerves: he was still passionately irritated, indignant, angry when critics attempted to rebut his arguments. One felt that a writer of his status should have replied to them, if at all, with brevity and calmness. The more entrenched his position became, the less he seemed to be able to bear attacks on it, however ill-aimed. He was, in his later years, too apt, one felt, to use such terms as 'second-rate minds', which, however well-deserved, were not worthy of his own powers of literary expression. His early writings were beautiful, without any of the explosive elements which occasionally jarred in some of the later ones and naturally provoked the second-rate minds to further offence. One longed to suggest a little blue-pencilling, but I never felt I could, and when I once asked Raleigh whether he could, he said no.

With an invitation to one of the All Souls' lunch parties the Doctor said: 'It'll be Palm Sunday, so bring your palm.' I went off to Burns, Oates and Washbourne, but they could not provide a single palm, only a sheaf; so I bought that and gave all the branches, except one, to a local church; the remaining one I coated with gold paint, which made it look most graceful and beautiful, like something from a medieval Italian painting. The study was so full on my arrival, the Doctor had only time to make a gesture of satisfaction, as if to say 'Good, that's right', before he stuck it up somewhere.

This was the occasion on which, in the train back to London, I was reading a learned journal containing a discussion between two incensed opposites, the Doctor on the one side, and Professor Trevor-Roper (later Lord Dacre) on the other. Despite their argument, Trevor-Roper was quoted as saying: 'Anyone who thinks he knows more about the Elizabethan period than Dr Rowse does had better be very careful of his step.'

Having mentioned the fiery impatience the Doctor occasionally showed, one must pay tribute to the wonderful change that came over his manner when he was treating you as one of his students. His extreme clarity of exposition – he was never at a loss for a word – and the authority of his vast store of knowledge was combined with a striking gentleness. One could see how effective, how inspiring he must have been as a tutor; not the less because he expected and demanded very hard work.

In one of his very early books, *The Spirit of English History*, Rowse had said one of the best things ever heard, I think, about Arthur: 'It was the hero of the losing side, King Arthur, who imposed himself on the imagination, the chief and lasting contribution of the Celts to the mind and literature of Europe.'

When I found that the firm thought well of my book, I asked the Doctor's permission to dedicate it to him. They had, of course, sent him a proof copy. To my delight he said that he would be glad to have dedicated what he called 'this interesting and original book'.

Thirteen

❦

Raleigh Trevelyn had now moved to the firm of Hamish Hamilton and in 1976 he suggested my writing about the Princes in the Tower. I at once fastened on to this idea.

The thought of the book led my steps to Westminster Abbey. I had been, briefly, at a boarding school (where I had not behaved at all well) of which my most valuable recollection is the teaching of a visiting history mistress, Miss Dorothea Price-Hughes. She was a little odd and eccentric and the other girls were inclined to make fun of her, in a good-natured way, behind her back, but I thought she was wonderful: what she told you conveyed a sense of vision and space.

Miss Price-Hughes once told us that after the Battle of Bosworth was won, and the crown had tumbled from the helmet of Richard III, a soldier had picked it up and hung it on the branch of a hawthorn bush, from which it was retrieved and placed on Henry Tudor's head, and that this was well attested. After all, she said, there is the stained glass window in Westminster Abbey, with the picture of the crown and the thorn bush. I never asked her to say where in the Abbey the window was; when, so many years later, I went to look for it, I assumed it must be in the chapel of Henry VII, but I could not find it.

A kind and cheerful retired naval officer, acting temporarily in the position of verger, came with me and agreed that it was not to be seen in the chapel. He said, however, that there were five small painted panes above one of the altars, so dusty that their figures were indecipherable from ground level; but, he added, there was scaffolding up against one of the west towers, with planks across it, which would lead one to the outside of the panes; if I liked, he would take me up there. I agreed eagerly. We went up several flights

[163]

of a stone staircase; on one of the landings a grim-looking old verger said to my guide: 'Are you bringing this lady up here on your own responsibility?' 'Yes, yes,' my guide said cheerfully. (It was a case of the Navy's here!) We came out on to a platform of planks which fortunately prevented me from realising the height at which we stood. A stiff breeze was blowing. A step or two and we were in front of the panes. They were, close up, dimmed but legible; but they showed heraldic devices only. My guide had one more shot in his locker: when we got back inside the tower, he took me into a large reading, or muniment room, on one of the upper floors, furnished with massive wooden tables at which several owl-like men in black gowns and large round spectacles were sitting. My guide explained what I was in search of; one or two of them murmured to each other and even opened volumes, but all to no purpose; they knew nothing of any such window. When we reached ground level again, I thanked him most warmly. I did not like to offer him a tip, I was afraid it might be the wrong thing. I wish now that I had risked it.

Despite this setback, I happened to mention my search to Renée Haynes, formerly Secretary of the Society for Psychical Research and a repository of all kinds of arcane and fascinating information. She obtained for me a photograph from the National Monuments Record of the glass of which Miss Price-Hughes had told us. It is not in Henry VII's main chapel, but in the east window of the East Apsidal Chapel, in which tall, narrow panes each carry a Tudor rose beside a bush, surmounted by a crown. The learned men working in the Abbey in their black gowns had never heard of the window, but it is there, just as Miss Price-Hughes had said it was.

The climax of the fearful story of the Two Princes in the Tower, the details of their lives and what is known, or supposed, about their deaths, is short in relation to the historical context of the rest of the book, but I felt the latter was of such gripping interest, all contributing to the realism of the scene, that I was unable to leave any of it out. Though everything I related was already in print, so much of it, as regarded details of clothes and living conditions in general, was found in very scholarly works: chief of these being C. L. Scofield's *The Life and Reign of Edward IV,* a monument of detailed, domestic research; but this was published in 1923. I also believed that the portrait of Elizabeth Woodville, Edward IV's queen, in the north transept of Canterbury Cathedral had not previously had justice done to it. There are portraits of the queen in miniatures on documents, but all of them, emphasising her yellow hair and the drooping of her heavy eyelids, give almost the impression of caricatures. Her figure in the family group of Edward IV, with the two princes and the five princesses, is of astonishing grace, elegance and fascination: the face, cold and sly, with the heavy eyelids, makes one see not a caricature, but a likeness. A Puritan vicar, in 1643, smashed the faces of all the figures except those of the king and queen, therefore all the faces except those of Edward IV and Elizabeth are eighteenth-century restorations.

While working on the book I had an interesting conversation with General Raeburn who was then the Resident Governor of the Tower. I raised the point made by Kendall that the Duke of Buckingham might have been responsible for the boys' murders, on the ground that he was possibly aiming at the Crown, and if this scheme was to succeed, it was essential first to remove Edward IV's two sons. General Raeburn said: 'Buckingham could not have got at the children, or sent murderers to them, unless the Governor of the Tower had connived at the scheme, and', he added, 'I don't think he'd have done it.' It was impressive to hear these words from such an authority in such a place.

As I made my way back from my interview with General Raeburn to the gateway, I passed two of the Tower's ravens, standing on a low parapet. Though I had of course heard of the existence of these famous birds, I had never seen one, and I had not realised before how tall a raven stands and with what massive shoulders.

When I was at work on this book, with a somewhat firm dateline, I had an offer from *Reader's Digest* to contribute to a collection of accounts of criminal investigation, illustrating the work of Scotland

Yard. The subjects had all to be dated not earlier than 1829, when the first headquarters of the Metropolitan Police Force was established in Scotland Yard. There were eight cases in this collection, all of them except mine dated in the twentieth century: mine ran from 1891 to 1892. The other seven were expositions of highly skilled detective work, forming a vivid intellectual picture, highly strung and hard-going, enthralling to read, but, for me, impossible to emulate.

My case was that of the poisoner Neill Cream. This I found congenial because the dates meant that one could actually see the London of the period, much of which was still standing in spite of air-raid damage, and everything one had read about life in late Victorian London seemed to occur to one's mind and make its revealing contribution. Neill Cream was a criminal of a bent of which I had never heard before. He persistently made contact with whores, and at parting with them he would give them three 'long, thin pills' which he assured them would do them good. These were capsules containing a lethal dose of strychnine, which brought on indescribable agonies and after a few hours ended in death; but what gave him exquisite pleasure was not the sight of their sufferings, for he was never present when these came on, but to hear of the fearful throes, the public commotion, the inquest, the burial. He would buy every newspaper of the dates that carried these, and read the facts over and over again, discussing them with people he knew and relating them to casual acquaintances.

A native of Illinois, Cream had, ten years before, spent some time in London studying for a degree at St Thomas's Hospital; he never sat for it, but on the strength of this he called himself Dr Neill. He had served a gaol sentence in America on a charge of poisoning, in the course of which he inherited the family money. The authorities allowed him considerable remission, and as soon as he came out he returned to London, to the delights of whoring in its small, dark streets which made such an exciting contrast to its splendid, stately buildings and its airy squares and open spaces, something he had never forgotten in all the suffering tedium of ten years in an American gaol. Now Dr Neill, MD, he adopted clothes of heavy respectability, including a caped greatcoat and a tall silk hat. He found desirable lodgings with Miss Sleaper at 103 Lambeth Palace Road. Past the gateway of Lambeth Palace, the London home of the Archbishop of Canterbury, and between it and the river stood the original buildings of St Thomas's Hospital; across the river were the Victorian Gothic towers of the Houses of Parliament. At the riverside end of Lambeth Palace Road was Westminster Bridge, and at the other end of the bridge stood an *Lambeth* opulent building, red-brick-faced with Portland stone, towers and turrets all with a striped, red and white Byzantine look. The building had been meant for an opera house but the founder's money had run out before the scheme was finished, so in 1890 it had been acquired by the Detective Branch of the Metropolitan Police. The latter had previously occupied cramped quarters in Whitehall Place, still known as Scotland Yard because it had provided accommodation for the grooms and horses of Scots courtiers visiting the court of England in the sixteenth century.

This district, housing the highest authorities in the realm of Church, medicine and government, fronted a region now in decay: noisy public houses, shops for second-hand clothes, unswept pavements and littered streets. The appearance of Dr Neill had a curious appropriateness to the district he haunted. Tall and broad, he was cross-eyed behind his gold-rimmed glasses. Not only was the front of his head bald, the back of this skull had a look of baldness showing through his lank hair. In spite of his caped greatcoat and his silk hat, his expression, to anyone who caught a glimpse of it, would have seemed to qualify him as the evil genius of the neighbourhood.

The most exciting feature of this work, for me, was going about on foot, in the district between Westminster Bridge and Newington Causeway, and discovering that the humble streets of the story were still there. Two of Neill's victims were lodged in Stamford Street, off the Waterloo Road, and it was here that the remarkable powers of observation of a trained policeman came into force. On his beat down Stamford Street at a late hour, Constable Comley saw a young woman saying goodnight to a man as she let him out of the door of No. 18: a man of curious appearance. When a few hours later he was called to the same house by a fellow constable, to attend to two young women screaming in the agonies of strychnine poisoning, he heard from one of them that a man called Fred had given her two long pills. He said: 'Was that the man I saw you letting out of the house two hours ago?' 'Yes,' she said. He and his fellow constable got the girls into a cab and took them to St Thomas's Hospital; one was dead on arrival, the other died in a few hours; but Constable Comley was able to give such a vivid description of the nocturnal visitor to his superior, Sergeant Wood, that the latter was able to identify him one evening in the crowd outside a public house at the end of Westminster Bridge Road, eyeing the women as they paraded up and down. Comley was on duty outside the Canterbury Music Hall. Wood sent a small street urchin with a message to him, and Comley arrived. 'That's him,' he said. At last their quarry went off with one of the women and they followed him, down St George's Road and then into a mean and ill-lit little street leading off it – Elliott's Row. There the couple turned into a house and the two policemen prepared themselves for a long vigil. It ended at last: the house door opened, and their quarry went off, stealthily followed by these two policemen, till he stopped at No. 103 Lambeth Road and let himself in with a key.

All this was morbidly exciting to read about, but it had never entered my head that one could actually see Elliott's Row – the terrain was distant and many small streets had been destroyed in the Blitz and afterwards rebuilt; but while I was working on this piece, I was visiting a friend in St Thomas's Hospital. As they wanted her to have hydrotherapy, she was transferred to Lambeth Hospital and I went there after her. On my going home it was dark, and as I came towards Newington Causeway I saw, first, in an otherwise empty and silent little street, a brilliantly lit shop-window, its only occupant a man planing the boards of a coffin, and then – I could hardly believe my eyes – a small street label: Elliott's Row!

I had not then developed my allergy to alcohol, but I had, even then, a very light head, so when *Reader's Digest* gave a party for us and we were met at the door with trays full of glasses of champagne, I took first one, and then another; after that I went bouncing round the room, shouting out conversational remarks to complete strangers. Of us eight writers, I was the only one in connection with whose subject there were, of course, no Scotland Yard men surviving. All the other seven had police authorities: detective superintendents, detective officers, who had been concerned with the cases assigned to them, to give them help and insight. I was, in one way, sorry to be the odd-man-out in this arrangement; I should have liked to have one of these calm and formidably knowledgeable men assigned to me, but it would have been a waste of valuable police time. What they could have told me of the facts was already in print; the rest of the matter I, and only I, could do for myself.

There was, for me, an interesting outcome of the *Great Cases of Scotland Yard* party. One of the directors of *Reader's Digest*, on seeing me off the premises, held my elbow and told me in a discreet tone of voice that he thought my contribution the best of the collection. My brother David said when I told him this, 'He probably went round the room saying that to everybody.' Well, perhaps; but I had, almost immediately afterwards, an invitation from another of them to have breakfast with him at Claridge's, to discuss a project which he thought might be profitable to both of us. I had heard of business breakfasts but had never attended one. This was very agreeable; unfortunately I hadn't the appetite to take any of the delicious dishes on offer, but the coffee was particularly good, and the toast was quite heavenly, like nothing I've had in the way of toast before or since. Meanwhile, the scheme propounded to me was to write a feature on the present Royal Family. Those fatally incongruous figures which afterwards became attached to the Royal Family had not then risen above the horizon and nothing was needed in the way of emotional colouring except sympathy and enthusiasm, but the project was out of my sphere. I had not the entrée, nor did I know anyone who had. He said: 'We could arrange all that for you', and I was sure they could: in their own way, they were very potent; but I knew it was not for me.

I have, over many years, been fascinated by the phenomenon of spiritualism and I now felt that, while I still had the energy, I should investigate it further. My researches led to my writing virtually my last book, the life of the medium, Daniel Dunglas Home, whose amazing career lasted from 1833 to 1888. Home was a medium who put members of his audience into communication with relatives or friends who had died. The complete conviction of the sitters of the genuineness of these communications, and the undoubted fact that over a long career Home was never detected in fraud, left no doubt in my mind as to his honesty. I only wondered whether the spirit communications might have been the result of telepathy, in which the sitter's vivid memory of the dead person might have transferred itself to the medium's mind, rather than that of the objective presence of the spirit. This, however, did not affect belief in Home's extraordinary psychic powers, among them that of levitation, of which he performed amazing feats, fully recorded by people who had been present at the scene, though violently denied by people who had not. I lived in this book while I was reading for it and writing it, in much the same way as I had in *Dr Gully*. When Home was dying, he wrote to a friend: 'I wait for the shadow that precedes the never-fading light.' I called the book *The Shadow and the Light*.

I sent a copy to Sir David Smithers, a friend who had been the Director of Radiotherapy at the Royal Marsden Hospital, where he had worked for forty years. Devoted to his profession, he was also ardently interested in literature and history. When he was at last at leisure, he wrote several books, of which, I suppose, the best known is *The Idle Trade*, a quotation from Pope's *'Epistle to Dr Arbuthnot'* – 'I left no calling for this idle trade'. The work is a collection of biographical essays on doctors who were also writers, among whom Keats and Somerset Maugham are perhaps the most unexpected. One is familiar with most of the names, but not with their fascinating works, discoveries and experiences.

David Smithers's reaction to my book was to send me a long and most interesting letter. He wrote:

> I have seen and marvelled at levitation ... I have only known one magician, and he did extraordinary things in my house for which I was quite unable to offer explanations. That Dunglas Home did these things so convincingly is fascinating, they ought to be accounted for, extraordinary explanations may be true. We have far more senses than we recognise, unconscious sense-organs abound in the body, action at a distance is well-known to psychics ... but why choose spiritualistic explanation as the most likely answer, on such slender evidence?
>
> This letter, I fear, getting too long, but I have only just reached the part which is of main interest to me. This is the problem of mind/body relationship. States of consciousness require corporeal foundations. We, as people, are slowly self-created ... we build ourselves out of our inheritance, upbringing and early education ... You could not separate mind from body and be left with either person ... I do not see how a spiritualistic theory ... is to be invalidated; it is a matter of faith and not one open to reason. The evidence for spirits is so nebulous, their contribution to our knowledge so trivial, and the mind/body separation so incredible, that judgement should be suspended until some satisfactory means of testing a spiritualistic interpretation can be devised ... That unexplained phenomena occur is part of human experience. Gaining experience through disciplined attacks on hypotheses, trying to disprove pet theories, is the main gateway to the emancipation of man.
>
> I hope you will take it as a compliment that your book should have provoked such a strenuous reaction.

I did take it as a compliment.

Epilogue

A few years ago I had two accidents, of which the second left me more or less housebound. I had to be removed from my house in Downshire Hill as I could no longer walk up and down stairs.

In compiling this memoir I have encountered many lapses of memory into the void. But the effort involved has wonderfully brought back the past, or part of it. Much of it I have altogether forgotten, but some episodes have come back of their own accord, with an almost supernatural vividness. The untimely deaths of my two brothers – Romilly from heart failure in 1969, and David by a fall in 1987 – have also made a chasm in actual experience; but memory and consciousness have assumed a sort of unearthly brightness.

I have put down what I hope may interest other people. Here and there I have used discretion because I feel it less painful to be abused for leaving things out than abused for putting things in. I have lost a good deal, but as Edith Sitwell says: 'In the end, all is harvest.'

When, after one my of my accidents, I was in hospital, I was asked if I would like to see the Catholic priest who called on any patients who would welcome a visit. I said yes. When I told him that 'Everybody belonging to me is dead', he said: 'Then they are all waiting to welcome you on the other side.' I had thought this, but received considerable comfort from hearing him say it. Henry Vaughan's poem 'To Friends Departed' says: 'They are all gone into the world of light.' A great many people do not believe this. I do not want to contend with them. I will add nothing.

Index